Daily Marriage Devotionals

FOR LIFETIME LOVERS

A Year of Encouraging Readings for Couples

Library of Congress Cataloging-in-Publication
Data is available upon request
ISBN 979-8-9860252-9-2
Printed in the United States

Unless otherwise identified, Scripture quotations are taken from the King James Version,
New King James Version, and New International Translation.

PurposePals

Published 2023 by PurposePals LLC
purposepalsllc.com

Welcome Lifetime Lovers,

Your life together is before you. Take hold of it and never let go. We pray that each nugget will be a blessing to you as an individual and your relationship with your spouse. We challenge you to re-evaluate your vows and covenant between you and God. Know that your marriage is ordained by Him and part of His original plan. A covenant marriage is not built on deceit, selfishness, materialism, or lust, but on a foundation that is built upon Godly principles, reflecting a relationship bound by unconditional love and respect.

We challenge you to keep "working" on your marriage; the work is constant. Cover each other in prayer and be supportive of one another. Let your children see God in you as you strive to build your family, with God being the center. Remember to keep dating and to "love hard." Keep us in your prayers as God opens a new chapter in our lives. Our prayer is that God is glorified in all that we do.

Blessing upon you both,
Danny and Rhoda Whitfield

INTRODUCTION

Growing together as a couple is a beautiful thing. There will be times of disagreements and things that occur that make you feel that you're on an impossible journey. But one of the most beautiful things about our God is that He is the very essence of love. Therefore, if you keep Him included in every facet of your marriage, you'll find yourselves experiencing a wonderful union. It's a must that you never exclude Him from the equation. When I consider how He puts up with us but He loves us despite our shortcomings, I can't help but love him more. He has seen us through many valleys. He tells us in Ephesians 5:25 (NIV) Husbands, love your wives, just as Christ loved the church and gave himself up for her. We can never love her too much. Love is not an emotion but an attitude. Your attitude in marriage will determine the mood of the love for your partner. It's not based on how you feel but a mindset that leads to a display of actions necessary to enhance your partner's life. Pray for the love of your marriage each day, that God will forever give you an attitude of love for your spouse. God demonstrated His love for us while we were sinners. What a great demonstration of love. Because of this, we should be willing to follow this excellent example as we share in our imperfections and yet find a way to love each other.

When you look at your mate, what do you see? You should see a partner for life, a lover and a friend. One who looks beyond your past and sees you becoming what God has designed you to be in your marriage. A husband and wife are ready and willing to work together in their marriage. Continue to love each other during the difficult moments and love each other with everlasting love. Love is not only spoken in words, but it's demonstrated by actions every day. So, as you travel through the "Daily Marital Nugget Devotional for Lifetime Lovers," you find enriching nuggets and scriptures to render you the daily encouragement you need to keep moving forward on your marital journey.

Place me like a seal over your heart, like a seal on your arm;
for love is as strong as death, its jealousy unyielding as the grave.
It burns like blazing fire, like a mighty flame.
Song of Solomon 8:6 (NIV)

Day 1

So, teach us to number our days, that we may gain a heart of wisdom.
Psalms 90:12(NKJV)

We can only live ONE day at a time. Therefore, allow God to bless your marriage each day. Remember that you can only change the issues of YOURSELF, not your spouse. Always remember not to waste time on PETTY matters in your marriage. Love each *other to the fullest every day because tomorrow is NOT promised.* Thereby, continue to love hard to have NO regrets: love your spouse as Christ loves YOU.

Personal Reflection

What can I gain from this nugget and scripture that will help me on my marital journey?

_____

_____

_____

_____

_____

_____

_____

_____

_____

Day 2

All scripture is God-breathed and is useful for teaching, rebuking, correction and training in righteousness, so that the servant of God may be thoroughly equipped for every good work.
II Timothy 3:16-17(NIV)

It's another day lifetime lovers. Vow to be committed to your marriage by having a long-term perspective or view of the relationship and a willingness to make sacrifices. Always be able to compromise and change your behaviors for the long-term good of the relationship. You must decide to stay in the marriage, in sickness and health, trusting that your partner will stay as well.

Personal Reflection
What changes can I make to improve ME?

_____

_____

_____

_____

_____

_____

_____

_____

_____

Day 3

Therefore, shall a man leave his father and mother, and shall cleave unto his wife:
and they shall become one flesh.
Genesis 2:24(KJV)

Change in your marriage is not an event but a process. Will you finish it, or will you be guilty of not seeing the process to the end? Two hearts that beat as one! One Heartbeat.

Personal Reflection

What can I do to be a part of the process of change in my marriage?

_____

_____

_____

_____

_____

_____

_____

_____

Day 4

Charity suffereth long, and is kind; charity envieth not; charity vaunteth not itself, is not puffed up, Doth not behave itself unseemly, seeketh not her own, is not easily provoked, thinketh no evil; Rejoiceth not in iniquity, but rejoiceth in the truth; Beareth all things, believeth all things, hopeth all things, endureth all things.
1 Corinthians 13:4-7(KJV)

Can you love your partner with an unconditional love? God cares for us so much that He loves us despite our faults and failure. Your love for each other makes a statement to the world that I love this person enough to give them all of me heart and soul, and to be exclusively bound to that person through a Holy union. Love hard.

Personal Reflection

God what am I to learn from this nugget and scripture?

_____

_____

_____

_____

_____

_____

Day 5

And now abideth faith, hope, charity, these three;
but the greatest of these is charity.
1 Corinthians 13:13(KJV)

Your love for each other transcends all barriers and obstacles that may come against you. It is not wavering but is constant. Love is the spiritual gift that each of you bring to the marriage. Love perseveres.

Personal Reflection

How does this nugget help me to define my love for my spouse?

_____

_____

_____

_____

_____

_____

_____

_____

Day 6

Wherefore comfort yourselves together, and edify one another, even as also ye do.
1 Thessalonians 5:11 (KJV)

So, what is patience? It's your marriage enduring difficult circumstances. Unexpected or unexplained events may take place and alter your life. There must be a willingness to wait patiently for things to work out. Waiting may seem awkward and uncomfortable, but if you wait patiently, your change WILL come! Loving your spouse through tough times and issues is essential. Being patient with them will go a long way in saving your marriage. Your marriage can be re-energized as both of you experience acceptance and encouragement during your PROCESS. Giving up your routine and humility is the best insurance to keep the marriage solid.

Hold it steady!!!!

Personal Reflection
How am I encouraged to be patient in my marriage?

_____

_____

_____

_____

_____

_____

Day 7

Therefore, what God has joined together, let not man separate.
Mark 10:9(NKJV)

It is inevitable that two people living together so close would not irritate or aggravate each other. In most situations, the irritated person has brought outside forces into the home. It could have been something that happened on the job, indifferences with another family member, lack of finances, or just a plain hard day at work. Even though your spouse may be short with you, it has nothing to do with you but something they experienced before having contact with you. James 3 tells us that every part of the body can be tamed, but not the tongue. Though the tongue is a small member of our body, it defiled the whole body because we allow it to become so unruly when irritated. With that being said, those outside forces have no place in going home with you.

Your spouse and family did not contribute to the mood that you are in and should not be the ones to feel the brunt of how your day went. You have to just talk out these things and get off your chest to avoid being unnecessarily ugly to your spouse unintentionally. You may not be able to tame the tongue, but you can choose to control it. God has blessed you with someone created and designed just for you. One to attend to your needs and desires, to listen and feel your pain. Your home should always be your refuge where you know someone with time, love and patience to listen to you. Let your love for your spouse always be laced with patience.

Personal Reflection
What am I to learn from this nugget and scripture?

_____

_____

_____

_____

_____

_____

_____

_____

_____

Personal Reflection
How can this nugget benefit how I communicate with my spouse?

_____

_____

_____

_____

_____

_____

_____

_____

_____

Day 8

Except the Lord build the house, they labour in vain that build it:
except the Lord keep the city, the watchman waketh but in vain.
Psalms 127:1(KJV)

When you're in love, you'll find practical steps to take your marriage from good to great. It's always important to check your marital vital signs. Is there a pulse? Like a garden needs nurturing, so does your marriage. Be sure to prioritize being intimate, romantic, and having fun together in your marriage.

Personal Reflection
How can I apply this nugget to my marriage?

_____

_____

_____

_____

_____

_____

_____

_____

Day 9

A soft answer turneth away wrath: but grievous words stir up anger.
Proverbs 15:1(KJV)

Love is patient. Love is kind. These words were recited in your wedding vows. Putting meaning behind these words and making love last is the hardest part. Marriage is something you work at; it's a job. It will not always be fun stuff. Being patient doesn't mean biting your tongue, but knowing what words to use and when. Always be careful with your words; some things you won't be able to take back. These two pillars, love and patience, are placed upon a prepared and well-planned foundation that can stand even when pressure is applied.

Personal Reflection

What can I learn from this nugget and scripture?

_____

_____

_____

_____

_____

_____

_____

Day 10

I waited patiently for the Lord; and He inclined unto me, and heard my cry.
Psalms 40:1(KJV)

To have patience means expressing the positive when you want to point out the negative. You have to make a conscious decision to overlook some things that are not very pleasant to you and think about the better days ahead. Knowing that you didn't divorce when you considered it but were determined to be patient instead, you can now celebrate good times, many anniversaries, and your lives together. Patience is an attribute of God. So, each time you find yourselves in situations where you must put patience to work, know that you are on the verge of "becoming."

Personal Reflection
How can I apply this nugget and how can it help my marriage?

_____

_____

_____

_____

_____

_____

_____

Day 11

Be careful for nothing; but in everything by prayer and supplication with thanksgiving let your requests be made known unto God.
Philippians 4:6(KJV)

Patience brings internal calm during an external storm. Trials may better your marriage and even test your patience. If you are committed to seeing your marriage through tough times, you must summons every ounce of strength you have. Your marriage is more than an act of love. It is an act of will. While many marriages end up scarred and damaged by life's storms, many do emerge stronger and smarter from the many lessons you've learned through your storms. Remember that with God, you can weather ANY storm.

Personal Reflection

How does this nugget help me when stress and storms come?

_____

_____

_____

_____

_____

_____

_____

Day 12

Who so keepeth his mouth and tongue keepeth his soul from troubles.
Proverbs 21:23(KJV)

Couples who learn to manage their rage must agree that it is necessary to express and acknowledge it. You should agree never to attack each other in anger even though you share angry feelings. You should agree with each other that you won't yell at one another. If you can create a non-yelling policy, it will remove the need for your spouse to feel defensive or to develop any retaliation. If both of you can express your offense calmly, you will be better able to find out how and why the anger, is present in your marriage. In the heat of anger so many things can be said that you can't take back.

This is an excellent time to refrain from speaking and choose to pray. It's not whether we get angry, but what we do with that anger that matters.

Personal Reflection
How can I apply this nugget as I work to improve communication in our marriage?

_____

_____

_____

_____

_____

_____

Day 13

Fulfill ye my joy, that ye be like-minded, having the same love,
being of one accord, of one mind.
Philippians 2:2(KJV)

Now let's bring patience into our marriages. Just what does that look like? It means taking time to listen to your spouse and interact with them when you need (by your definition) to be doing something else. It means not getting upset when your spouse is late showing up. It means taking the time to explain something to your spouse that you know and they want to know. It means putting them before you. It means doing all the above and more without getting angry or upset. It is daily living out James 1:19 with your spouse: "Everyone should be quick to listen, slow to speak, and slow to become angry." Patience. Please find it and put it in your marriage.

Personal Reflection
God what am I to learn from this nugget and scripture?

_____

_____

_____

_____

_____

_____

_____

Day 14

A wrathful man stirreth up strife: but he that is slow to anger appeaseth strife.
Proverbs 15:18(KJV)

One of the ways we imitate God in our marriage is to be slow to anger and to abound with great love toward each other. You may say that you love your spouse. Well, I do too, but our love should show itself in many ways, and one should be with our attitude, behavior, and our words. If we would sum it up in a word, it would be the word that we have been discussing this week and last week - patience. Patience is one of the nine fruit of the Spirit and sometimes the most challenging for us to walk in when we face trying times within our marriage. God is our example. He is patient with us because He loves us so much that He slows His anger down. Just for that, I am eternally grateful! Are you?

Personal Reflection
How can I better demonstrate my love to my spouse? How does this nugget speak to me?

_____

_____

_____

_____

_____

_____

Day 15

Wherefore they are no more twain, but one flesh. What therefore
God hath joined together, let not man put asunder.
Matthew 19:6(KJV)

Everyone wants the perfect relationship and the perfect marriage. Guess what? There is no such thing as a perfect person, relationship, or marriage. We all have flaws, and every couple is going to have shortcomings. However, you can turn those flaws and weaknesses into a beautiful lasting marriage. Love is wonderful and beautiful, but marriage is about more than love. It is about working together as a team and accepting each other as perfectly imperfect.

Personal Reflection

How can I better learn from our individual differences? Can I accept my spouse for who they are?

_____

_____

_____

_____

_____

_____

_____

Day 16

See that none renders evil for evil unto any man;
but ever follow that which is good, both among yourselves, and to all men.
1 Thessalonians 5:15(KJV)

Love is the joy that comes from God when we care about the benefit of God and the use of another person more than our self. Love in a marriage says I am committed to you, I care about you, I have your best interest in mind, I want you to be happy, what matters to you also matters to me, AND I want to help you to be the best person you can be. When you make your partner your priority, you won't have time to focus on evil for evil.

Personal Reflection

How can I better express my love and commitment to my spouse?

_____

_____

_____

_____

_____

_____

_____

Day 17

Doth not behave itself unseemly, seeketh not her own,
is not easily provoked, thinketh no evil.
I Corinthians 13:5(KJV)

Consider the great example the Word gives us on the subject of love. Love is patient, love is kind. It does not envy, it does not boast, it is not proud. It does not dishonor others, it is not self-seeking, it is not easily angered, it keeps no record of wrongs. Love does not delight in evil but rejoices with the truth. 7 It always protects, always trusts, always hopes, always perseveres 1 Corinthians 13:4-7(NIV). It (Love) will NEVER fail. This passage of scripture gives us new meaning to the words "I love you." What does this type of love look like, and what does it say? Baby, I love you. What I'm saying is that I will be patient and kind to you. I will not be jealous of you, I will not be boastful in your presence. I promise never to be rude to you; I will see your good and not mine. I won't be easy to get mad, and I will not keep a record of your faults. What if we could love in this way ALL THE TIME. Today might be a good day to start. Remember, we like our marriages, are a "work in progress." Press on!!

Personal Reflection
What are ways that I can better communicate my love to my spouse?

_____

_____

_____

_____

_____

Day 18

Wherefore, my beloved brethren, let every man be swift to hear,
slow to speak, slow to wrath.
James 1:19(KJV)

Has your spouse ever asked you to do something significant, but you misunderstood the exact meaning of what needed done and you did it differently? Has your spouse ever talked to you about their feelings, but you weren't listening, and so you didn't understand them and what they meant? This can be frustrating and fuel the fire for anger and silent treatment. We are commanded to treat others in the same manner we want to be treated. If we remember this is what God desires of us, to be considerate and kind to our spouse.

It is insulting to shun or make fun of the feelings and thoughts of those whose opinions differ from ours. Instead of doing this, first try to be more understanding of their feelings. That will help you to be more apt to HEAR. Listening to your spouse is a MUST in your marriage. Compassion and respect will follow. "I hear what you're saying baby."

Personal Reflection
God, what am I to learn from this nugget and scripture?

_____

_____

_____

_____

_____

_____

_____

_____

_____

_____

_____

_____

_____

Personal Reflection
How can I better demonstrate that, "I hear you?"

_____

_____

_____

_____

_____

_____

_____

Day 19

Hereby perceive we the love of God, because He laid down His life for us:
and we ought to lay down our lives for the brethren.
I John 3:16(KJV)

The most critical skill in maintaining unity as a couple is being able to forgive. You will undoubtedly make mistakes, disappoint one another, and even make bad decisions. The only way to keep the relationship growing in the midst of what we go through is to be able to forgive. The love you should have for each other should emulate the love God has for us. He loves us despite our shortcomings, even to the point of being forgettable.is a MUST in your marriage. Compassion and respect will follow.

Personal Reflection

How is God's love manifested in me as I show love to my spouse?

_____

_____

_____

_____

_____

_____

_____

Day 20

Let not mercy and truth forsake thee: bind them about thy neck;
write them upon the table of thine heart.
Proverbs 3:3(KJV)

Kindness is an essential ingredient in a healthy and happy marriage. Marriages are strengthened when both members of a marriage treat each other kindly: with love and understanding and with dignity and respect. Kindness is evident when a person puts the needs of their spouse first, acting on what will please or help the other most, and not on self-interest. By never being rude or abusive to your spouse in any way, you build a relationship of mutual trust and respect.

By demonstrating kindness or giving a gentle response to an angry statement, you let kindness wrap you and your thoughts in a blanket of respect that will smother the flames of anger before it rears its head. By doing this, kindness will be the product of your happiness.

Personal Reflection

How am I demonstrating kindness as I continue to love my lover for life?

_____

_____

_____

_____

_____

Day 21

Be ye therefore merciful, as your Father also is merciful.
Luke 6:36(KJV)

There should never be a night that you close your eyes and have not reconciled with your partner. Life is short and uncertain. Whatever is wrong, make it right, for we never know when our time is up. Forgive, Make Things Right. Fix it, clean it up, do what it takes to correct the mistake. Although you can't change the past, you can avoid making the same mistake in the future. Learn from your mistakes. Start the healing process and move forward.

Personal Reflection
How can I apply this nugget to my marriage?

_____

_____

_____

_____

_____

_____

_____

_____

Day 22

Husbands, love your wives,
even as Christ also loved the Church, and gave Himself for it.
Ephesians 5:25(KJV)

When you're away from your spouse, do you find yourself daydreaming or thinking about them? True love focuses on the other person, with your greatest concern being happiness and their well-being. Love does not decrease when two partners are separated from one another. Being in love is a continuous process; the personality, the romance, and your actions are all part of making your partner your "soul" mate. In your interactions and communication, there is a "knowing" of what each of you mean to each other. Continue the "process."

Personal Reflection
Based on your marital journey, how does today's nugget impact you?

_____

_____

_____

_____

_____

_____

_____

Day 23

Let us not love in word or in tongue, but in deed and in truth.
John 3:18(NKJV)

Most of us practice random acts of kindness toward our spouse on major holidays, birthdays, and anniversaries. But we need to remember to extend that courtesy to our beloved throughout the year and on other least important days. We sometimes expect love to take care of itself over time. We forget that love needs tending to if it is to remain in bloom. Practice regularly small and simple gestures that show support to your partner. Suggestions: Men - take a night or two and prepare dinner or order dinner. Get the kids ready for bed, assist with homework while your lady rest. Ladies - show up at work and take your husband out for lunch or treat him to a massage. The operative word is "practice." 1 John 3:18 says, "Let us not love in word or in tongue, but in deed and in truth."

Personal Reflection

God what am I to learn from this nugget and scripture? How can I best "show love?"

_____

_____

_____

_____

_____

_____

Day 24

The heart of the righteous studies how to answer:
but the mouth of the wicked pours forth evil.
Proverbs: 15:28(NKJV)

The Word of God tells us that the tongue can positively or negatively affect us. In our marriage, we must be careful how we respond to our mate; even in the heat of anger we recognize our target. They are our soul mate and we should be in the business of building and not tearing down. Remember, once it's said, it can't be taken back. Meditate and consider these scriptures. Pray about how they may change how you communicate in your marriage. A gentle answer turns away wrath, but a harsh word stirs up anger. Proverbs 15:1(NKJV) The soothing tongue is a tree of life, but a perverse tongue crushes the Spirit. Proverbs 15:4(NIV). Remember, the temperature of your marriage is gauged by what is being said.

Personal Reflection
God, what am I to learn from this nugget and scripture?

_____

_____

_____

_____

_____

_____

Day 25

Now the God of patience and consolation grant you to be likeminded one toward another according to Christ Jesus: That ye may with one mind and one mouth glorify God, even the Father of our Lord Jesus Christ.
Romans 15:5-6(KJV)

There is a phrase that says, "we're in this thing together." Well, you are!! Teamwork in a relationship means you combine your resources, time, efforts, and your goals in order to see your relationship prosper and move forward in unison. For example, doing household chores together, rather than relying on your partner, is a great way to spend extra time together and work as a team. Your relationship truly becomes about both of you and requires you both to participate daily to keep it moving forward and growing stronger.

Personal Reflection
God, what am I to learn from this nugget and scripture?

_____

_____

_____

_____

_____

_____

Day 26

Now I beseech you, brethren, by the name of our Lord Jesus Christ,
that ye all speak the same thing, and that there is no divisions among you;
but that ye be perfectly joined together in the same mind and in the same judgment.
I Corinthians 1:10(KJV)

It is possible that every person would say they are a good listener. But listening is not an innate ability all people possess; it's a skill we need to nurture. And it's a critical one for couples because the foundation of successful communication is truly listening to each other, without constructing a counter argument in your head. Always remember that it takes two to tango. There are two of you engaged and two components in that conversation; the one talking and the one actively listening. Check yourself. How does this impact you and your communication with your mate?

Personal Reflection

How can I improve my listening skills to clearly hear my spouse?

_____

_____

_____

_____

_____

_____

Day 27

From whom the whole body, joined and knit together by what every joint supplies,
according to the effective working by which every part does its share,
causes growth of the body for the edifying of itself in love.
Ephesians 4:16(NKJV)

Love is more than just mere words. It is more than an occasional gift. Love is a commitment to another person that shows itself in our willingness to adapt to and cooperate together. True love requires daily hard work. When we first started dating someone we were delighted that someone noticed and cared about us. Every gift was cherished. However, as the years passed, it required more than any old gift to show genuine love. But, if we have been paying attention, we know more about what is important to our partner. We become better at loving them. As you discover how to show best your love for your spouse, think over your relationship history. When have you felt closest to each other? When has each of you felt most loved by the other? How can you build such relationship-building time into your relationship now? Take the time and have that discussion with your spouse.

Personal Reflection
God what am I to learn from this nugget and scripture?

_____

_____

_____

_____

_____

_____

_____

_____

_____

_____

Personal Reflection
How can we better connect?

_____

_____

_____

_____

_____

_____

_____

_____

Day 28

She openeth her mouth with wisdom; and on her tongue is the law of kindness.
Proverbs 31:26(NKJV)

The Bible describes a woman whose husband and children bless and praise her. Among her noble attributes are these: "She opens her mouth with wisdom, and on her tongue is the law of kindness." Proverb 31:26(NKJV) The heart of a woman is to nurture and feed her family physically and spiritually. She exhibits kindness daily as she teaches how to be kind to others through her acts of service in the home. She is not weary in well-doing, and she delights to serve her family because she knows that out of the small things proceedeth that which is great. However, being selfless doesn't mean she must give up her own inner identity. God grants her the inner strength to attend to her family and herself. It is because of this that her husband and children bless and praise her.

Personal Reflection

If I am a woman, how can I best exhibit the attributes of a godly and virtuous woman? But if I am a man, how can I appreciate the attributes of a godly and virtuous woman?

_____

_____

_____

_____

_____

_____

Day 29

Mercy and truth are met together; righteousness and peace have kissed each other.
Psalms 85:10(KJV)

When you love your spouse, you should make decisions to act and treat them in a special way. It should be more on the actions you intend to show than you feel. Love is the promise, you and your partner made on your wedding day. It was the pledge you made, a source of security. For this reason, you promised to love and cherish each other for all eternity. If you can remember, you both did not promise to feel a certain way. Instead, the promise and the vow you made were sealed with the words for better or for worse. If you want to show your spouse that you love them, express it through your acts of kindness and gifts of affection. Acts of kindness will show that you love them, while gifts of affection show that you understand them. Your acts of kindness are never expected but will always be remembered.

Personal Reflection
How can this nugget help in stabilizing our marriage and its longevity?

_____

_____

_____

_____

_____

_____

_____

Day 30

Charity suffereth long, and is kind.
1 Corinthians 13:4(KJV)

What is it that you look for in your spouse? You should see someone with your best interest in mind, your biggest fan, and as someone once said, "the one that makes my liver quiver." They are the motivation that drives your marriage. With love like this, kindness would not be hard to show. It is not only expected but a reflection of our God, who demonstrates his loving-kindness to us each day. The Word says, "each morning brings with it brand new mercies." Show kindness to your soul mate. Your marriage won't last without it.

Personal Reflection
How can this nugget help me to reflect the character of God?

_____

_____

_____

_____

_____

_____

_____

Day 31

And they twain shall be one flesh: so then they are no more twain, but ONE flesh.
Mark 10:8(KJV)

I consider our marriage a partnership. My devotion is to make my spouse my number one priority. Their happiness is more important to me than my personal desires. Each day, we should honor the one God has blessed us to live our lives with. Honor them by listening to the events of their day, whether good or bad. Remember that our devotion to each other is vital to the growth of our marriages. We make each other "whole." Being devoted means drawing on each other in our strengths and weaknesses. With each day, we become each other's "priority." I am, because of you!

Personal Reflection
God, what am I to learn from this nugget and scripture?

_____

_____

_____

_____

_____

_____

_____

Day 32

My beloved is mine, and I am his: he feedeth among the lilies.
Until the daybreak, and the shadows flee away, turn, my beloved,
and be thou like a roe or a young hart upon the mountains of Bether.
Song of Solomon 2:16-17(KJV)

Marriage is never about any one of us. It involves each partner taking the back seat and putting each other first. When we can remove the me, my, and I in marriage and resort to meeting the needs of our mate, our marriages will last. Never allow selfish behavior into your marriage. It is in opposition to what a marriage should be about, that thing called LOVE.

Personal Reflection
How has this nugget help me to reflect on myself and my marriage?

_____

_____

_____

_____

_____

_____

Day 33

O house of Israel, cannot I do with you as this potter? Saith the Lord. Behold,
as the clay is in the potter's hand, so are ye in mine hand, O house of Israel.
Jeremiah 18:6(KJV)

Each of us brings to the marriage our imperfections and flaws. Don't make it a habit of pointing out each other's shortcomings. Know that each of you, brings something unique to your marriage, even with your flaws. Never try to change your mate to meet your specifications. Change can only come through prayer and that change will come within you first. What is important is that God has orchestrated your union and you should love each other just the way you are.

Personal Reflection
What does God want me to learn from this nugget and scripture?

_____

_____

_____

_____

_____

_____

_____

Day 34

Trust in the Lord with all thine heart; and lean not to thine own understanding.
In all thy ways acknowledge Him, and He shall direct thy paths.
Proverbs 3:5-6(KJV)

Choosing to make your spouse's happiness your priority is a great challenge. In our marriages, many things can sometimes cause us to lose focus of our commitment to each other. These include our careers, personal desires, and, yes even our children. There should never be a time when we take each other for granted. Now is a time that we look at our relationships and marriages and ask the question, what things have been placed ahead of the happiness of my spouse and my marriage?

Personal Reflection

How can I reflect and apply this nugget to my marital experience?

_____

_____

_____

_____

_____

_____

_____

Day 35

And let us not be weary in well-doing:
for in due season we shall reap, if we faint not.
Galatians 6:9(KJV)

Your commitment to your spouse means more than life itself. You will lose yourself for the cause of each other's happiness. The success of your marriage should be to live with expectations to fulfill the desires and dreams of your mate. If you have lost the fire, learn to love again. Start kissing. Kissing ignites the fire!!!

Personal Reflection
How has this nugget impacted you and your urgency to work your marriage?

_____

_____

_____

_____

_____

_____

_____

Day 36

Let nothing be done through strife or vain glory; but in lowliness
of mind let each esteem other better than themselves.
Philippians 2:3(KJV)

Try never to do anything with selfish intent. You should always be in a spirit of love. We should take on the mind and attitude of Christ. Our goal is not to "be served", but to "serve." We should have one purpose and intent, which is my partner's best interest for life.

Personal Reflection
What could I learn from this nugget and scripture?

_____

_____

_____

_____

_____

_____

_____

_____

Day 37

How precious also are Your thoughts to me, O God! How great is the sum of them!
If I should count them, they would be more in number than the sand;
when I awake, I am still with you.
Psalms 139:17-18(NKJV)

It's essential to always keep in the forefront of your mind why you should never take for granted your spouse's presence in your life. Life is like a vapor. Here today, gone tomorrow. Why are you thankful for your husband?

Spouse's Prayer

Most gracious and heavenly father, we come before you as humbly as we know how. We are thankful for those things that are the closest to us. So, we thank you for life, health, and strength. We thank you for blessing us with our marriages. Thank you for the person you blessed me to love and spend my life with. God, I ask that you continue to shower our marriages with your grace and mercy. As a married couple, we know that we will experience storms in our marriage, but we know as long as we stay close to you, you will bring us peace, encouragement, and strength to endure the test that you have before us. My prayer is that I can be a better spouse, a more loving partner who always shows compassion toward my lover for life. Help me to see things through my spouse's eyes and guide me to respond gently to them so that I can understand what they may be going through. I pray that you keep our marriage holy, fulfilled, and joyful. God bless us as a couple. Bless me to be the spouse you have called me to be. Equip us with everything we need spiritually, physically, morally, and financially. Bless our family and our home. This is my prayer today and forever. Amen.

Personal Reflection

How can this nugget impact our marriage and relationship?   How important is prayer to the marriage?

_____

_____

_____

_____

_____

_____

_____

_____

_____

_____

_____

_____

_____

_____

_____

Day 38

How precious also are Your thoughts to me, O God! How great is the sum of them!
If I should count them, they would be more in number than the sand;
when I awake, I am still with you.
Psalms 139:17-18(NKJV)

As a spouse, I am moved to be thankful for so many things. Most of all, I am grateful for a partner who has put up with me daily, with all my flaws, faults, and failures. Who also continues to be the vein of my being. I'm thankful for my biggest fan and the greatest supporter I have been blessed to have. When you feel that no one's in your corner, I can ALWAYS know that my spouse is there. The Bible tells us we should "give thanks in everything." Not only when things are well, but arguments, financial strain, or when we are struggling with our issues. I can genuinely say that despite all our ups and downs, good and bad days, I would not change a thing or choose to share my life with no one else. They say opposites attract. With God's help, my spouse has helped to pull some stuff out of me that I never knew existed. We are good for each other. I see them as "my gift", and the Word tells us that every good and perfect gift comes from Him. This is my lover, my soul mate, and the one that "makes my liver quiver." I am grateful for what we have shared and we are still experiencing today. And for this, I am truly thankful. Be thankful today for the gift that you've been given. Cherish them, and with each new day, glory in knowing they will share your deepest feelings and the many happy days ahead. Always take the time to tell your spouse how thankful you are for them being a part of your life.

Spouse's Prayer

Lord, I give thanks for your blessings and favor. I thank you for my mate and our family. I pray for your divine hand on our marriage and that you cover us with your grace. Bless every area of our lives as we continue to live together and grow in our love affair. Never let a day go by that I am not thankful for my spouse. God, thank you for this union you have ordained and sanctioned. God, I thank you for all my spouse does for me, the children, and my family. I thank you for blessing me with a beautiful companion, helpmate, and best friend. In Jesus Name Amen.

Personal Reflection

What can I do to show my gratitude to my lover for life? How important is it to pray for each other?

_____

_____

_____

_____

_____

_____

_____

_____

_____

_____

_____

Day 39

Giving thanks always for all things unto God and the Father in
the name of our Lord Jesus Christ;"
Ephesians 5:20 (KJV)

Each day you share with your spouse is a day to celebrate because it is a day that God has allowed us to experience when he blessed us with our spouse. Focus on learning to appreciate and treasure each day God allows you to have with your spouse because we don't know how many days we will have. Therefore, let's not waste time and energy on things that we can sit down and talk about. We already know the devil doesn't want us together, and he will do whatever possible to keep us apart. We have to recognize the enemy and face him head-on with the truth of God. Remember, God is not the author of confusion, but He is the author of love, peace, joy, and happiness. When we learn to appreciate each other and count our blessings, our whole life will turn around. Start counting your daily blessings and watch Him turn your lives around.

Personal Reflection
What can I learn from today's marital nugget?

_____

_____

_____

_____

_____

_____

_____

_____

_____

_____

_____

Personal Reflection

What can I do to show my gratitude to my lover for life? How important is it to pray for each other?

_____

_____

_____

_____

_____

_____

_____

_____

_____

Day 40

In everything give thanks: for this is the will of God in Christ Jesus concerning you.
I Thessalonians 5:18(KJV)

As you reflect on those things you are thankful for, it's also a time for you to take a self-inventory of where you are in your marriages or relationships and be grateful for the "process". I believe everything we encounter in life is a part of God's design. Your marriage is a part of God's design. The bumps, twists and turns, the ups and downs, are all part of His shaping and molding process. We should also be thankful. Because we both love God, I am genuinely grateful to know that things will "work together for our good."

We are often, only thankful for the good times and never for times of adversity. But we can rejoice in adversity, knowing that it's all a part of God's plan. Be thankful for all your marriage encompasses, and the mate He has designed for you. All of our days together have not been easy, but because of our love for each other He has taught us to love despite flaws and differences.

In time, He will blend two hearts as one. Therefore, remain grateful for the process. So today, take an inventory of YOU and reflect on where He has brought you, what He has brought you through, and yet be thankful. Scripture tells us that "in everything" we ought to give thanks. Thank Him for the "process".

Personal Reflection
God, how can I better demonstrate my love and appreciation to my spouse?

_____

_____

_____

_____

_____

_____

_____

_____

_____

Personal Reflection
What can I gain from this nugget and scripture to help me on my marital journey?

_____

_____

_____

_____

_____

_____

_____

Day 41

Set me as a seal upon thine heart, as a seal upon thine arm: for love is strong as death; jealously is cruel as the grave: the coals thereof are coals of fire, which hath a most vehement flame.
Songs of Solomon 8:6(KJV)

When you have thoughts of your mate, it should bring a smile to your face. The thoughts of good times and sensual times that might raise your eyebrows. We should marvel at the thought of waking each morning with the one you chose to love for the rest of your life. Thinking I wouldn't trade a day without my mate. Whatever your particular thoughts are for your mate, take the time to share them with them. I love you because ... Every thought that comes to mind should be a special one. It will help to rekindle the flame.

Personal Reflection
How can I reflect on today's nugget and apply it to my marriage?

_____

_____

_____

_____

_____

_____

_____

Day 42

Thy lips, O my spouse, drop as the honeycomb: honey and milk are under thy tongue;
and the smell of garments is like the smell of Lebanon.
Song of Solomon 4:11(KJV)

Your thoughts reflect your feelings for the one you love and who loves you. Reflect now on what made you fall in love with your mate. What was it that made you fall in love with them? Was it the curve of her hips, the warmth of his touch, or the kiss of the lips? These thoughts tell us that we've found the right fit, though flawed, but the missing piece to our "love" puzzle. I found this Hallmark card quote to be quite fitting; "I love you, not because you are perfect, but that you are perfect for me." Text your mate today and let them know thoughts you have for them when you are away from them. Leave a message to express how in love you are with them.

Personal Reflection
How can you relate this to your marriage?

_____

_____

_____

_____

_____

_____

_____

Day 43

The Lord is my strength and my shield; my heart trusted in Him, and I am helped: Therefore, my heart greatly rejoiceth; and with my song will I praise him.
Psalms 28:7(KJV)

It is always good to relish the thoughts of precious moments that you shared. Even the down times are good to remember because they remind us what you've experienced and endured together. Our thoughts are reflections of our past and hopes for days to come. Take the time together and reflect on how far you've come together. Revisit the not-so-happy times, but think about how the love you have for each other helped you through the worst and the best of times.

There is a song that my wife and I sang to each other on the day of our wedding that goes like this:

All the good times that we had always made up for the bad, Together the two of us
All the good times yet to come, all the things we haven't done, We'll share them the two of us
And when trouble comes to call, if we take another fall, I know we'll get through it all.
We'll be there the two of us; and when life is through with us, Those who knew of us will remember the two of us...

(Google Marilyn McCoo and Billy Davis - "The Two of Us" and take a listen.)

Personal Reflection
God what can I take from this nugget and scripture and apply to my marriage?

_____

_____

_____

Day 44

And the Lord God said, it is not good that the man should be alone;
I will make him an help meet for him.
Genesis 2:18(KJV)

God designed man to be a social creation, and He knew that man could not communicate with the animals. So, in His infinite wisdom, He created the best companion man could have in a woman. She would be the one whom we would take sweet counsel in and who could not only return the affection but would take an interest in our every endeavor.

I'm thankful for my partner for life and the comfort of knowing that I have a mate that was specifically designed for me to fulfill my desires as well as share in my successes and failures. We were meant for each other.

Personal Reflection
God, what am I to learn from this nugget and scripture?

_____

_____

_____

_____

_____

_____

Day 45

Beloved, let us love one another: for love is God; and every
one that loveth is born of God, and knoweth God.
I John 4:7(KJV)

Can your partner say to you that they feel loved? Yes, we might say to them that we love them, but it is very seldom demonstrated. Love is an action word. For women, it is really important for them to know that the husband loves them. We men think that it isn't necessary, but the romance in your marriage is an ongoing process. It never stops. So, let's keep the home fire burning. Turn up the heat in your love life!! It's on!!!

Personal Reflection
How can I apply today's nugget to my marriage?

_____

_____

_____

_____

_____

_____

Day 46

Wherefore comfort yourselves together, and edify one another, even as also ye do.
I Thessalonians 5:11(KJV)

We must recognize that we are two different individuals with two different thought processes. We must respect our differences and appreciate what each of us brings to the table. When we try to change our partners to think or act as we are, we take away their uniqueness of being who they are. Love and respect them for it. As one speaking from experience, when our personalities and thoughts mesh during marriage, you will find yourselves having the same thought patterns. Even when we may differ in how we see things in our marriage, we can still honor each other by ensuring that your opinions do not become an argument. Can you still love and respect your partner even though they don't think like you?

Personal Reflection
As I self-reflect, how can I apply this nugget to my marriage?

_____

_____

_____

_____

_____

_____

Day 47

I said, I will take heed to my ways, that I sin not with my tongue:
I will keep my mouth with a bridle, while the wicked is before me.
Psalms 39:1(KJV)

The power of life and death is in the tongue. It's amazing that the pink tornado can cause so much havoc. In a marriage, we must be cautious that what we say doesn't damage what we are trying to build. If what you are about to say is going to be damaging, it should be withheld. You must be careful to think things out before speaking because what you say can never be retracted from your spouse's mind. It's there to stay, sometimes, no matter how much we say I'm sorry.

So, ask God daily to bridle your tongue. In my marriage, I want to do all I can to edify; to build up my spouse and to be sure that what I say is NEVER damaging to my love and respect for them. You may be hurt by many people's words, but it hurts worse when it comes from your partner for life. Instead of saying something negative, point out their strengths. "Baby, I love how you. . ." or "Sweetie, you make feel so good when you . . ." "I love you because . . ." Find at least three positive things that you can say to compliment your spouse each day.

Personal Reflection
God, what am I to learn from this nugget and scripture?

_____

_____

_____

_____

_____

_____

_____

_____

_____

_____

_____

Personal Reflection
How has this nugget impacted and spoken to you today?

_____

_____

_____

_____

_____

_____

_____

Day 48

Let the word of Christ dwell in you richly in all wisdom; teaching and admonishing one another in psalms and hymns and spiritual songs, singing with grace in your hearts to the Lord.
Colossians 3:16(KJV)

There are certain things that are necessary for your mate to feel loved. What are some things that we could do to demonstrate that we love our partner? It's always good to do the unexpected. We must be careful that love doesn't take the back seat in our marriages. Whatever it took to woo our mate should be a continuous process. Send them a text or an email occasionally to let them know you're thinking of them. Every birthday, anniversary, or holiday should be days we pour it on.

Many times, it's not the quantity but the quality of thought. For those of you with children, plan a special day for your spouse. Pick up the children, help them with their homework, prepare them for bed, or plan a date with the grandparents and grands so you can be alone. Going on a date is not just for the young at heart, but to help keep the home fire burning for those that have been married for years. Make those plans today.

Personal Reflection

How can I use today's nugget to enhance our love for each other and apply the suggestions as we grow together?

_____

_____

_____

_____

_____

_____

_____

_____

_____

Personal Reflection
How has this nugget impacted and spoken to you today?

_____

_____

_____

_____

_____

_____

_____

_____

Day 49

Be anxious for nothing, but in everything by prayer and supplication,
with thanksgiving, let your requests be made known to God;
and the peace of God, which surpasses all understanding,
will guard your hearts and minds through Christ Jesus.
Philippians 4:6-7(NKJV)

Whatever you give out will eventually come back to you. It is so important that you honor the one you love without speaking words that may be damaging or hurtful. Promise to refrain from rude behavior that may turn into resentment and disharmony. Make sure you realize that you represent each other privately and publicly. There is a saying that "if you can't say something nice, don't say nothing at all." Any marriage where couples spend their time being rude and not considerate of each other is "toxic." When you see your relationship becoming miserable, and you can't enjoy each other's company, it's time to break and take a long hard look at your marriage. It's praying time. Know that the enemy's job is to destroy the sanctity of marriage. Stay on your watch and be able to identify his tactics. Keep the "main thing- the main thing" (each other); remember to love and cherish till death do us part.

Personal Reflection
How can I apply this nugget to my marriage?

_____

_____

_____

_____

_____

_____

_____

_____

_____

_____

Personal Reflection
How has this nugget caused me to think and reflect on my marital experience?

_____

_____

_____

_____

_____

_____

_____

Day 50

He that blesseth his friend with a loud voice, rising early in the morning,
it shall be counted a curse to him.
Proverbs 27:14(KJV)

This Proverb says that, if you chose to wake each morning with shouting rather than a pleasant "good morning", it would seem more of a curse than a blessing.

It's not what we say all the time, it's how we say it. We should clothe our words with gentleness. Every morning you have an opportunity to open your eyes is a blessing. Take that time and share that blessing with your partner with a word of thanks to God for another day that He has allowed you to spend with the one you love. Begin each day with words of encouragement, praying that God will order your steps as you go about your daily way of work. Begin it with a PRAISE!!

Personal Reflection

God, what am I to learn from this nugget and scripture?

_____

_____

_____

_____

_____

_____

Day 51

Render therefore to all their dues: tribute to whom tribute is due; custom to whom custom: fear to whom fear; honour to whom honour.
Romans 13:7(KJV)

So many times, we give honor, respect, and courtesy to everyone but those who are dear to us. We forsake those we are committed to, and they almost never receive our consideration. There are many ways for us to be considerate of our mates:

1. Never, ever make a decision that involves your family without considering your partner.
2. Be considerate when the ideas, opinions, or thoughts of your mate are presented to you.
3. Be considerate in thinking of the way we respond to our mates, even in times of disagreement.

When we are considerate of each other, we are seriously committing to our genuine love for each other. When we are kind to each other, we will begin to "shift" the atmosphere of our homes.

Personal Reflection
How can this nugget help change the communication atmosphere in my marriage?

_____

_____

_____

_____

Day 52

Being confident of this very thing, that he which hath begun a good work
in you will perform it until the day of Jesus Christ.
Philippians 1:6(KJV)

Mutual love is the desire of each of you to be together. You desire to be in each other's presence. This means we do things to create that atmosphere and not initiate situations or speak things that make tension. You will find that there will be times when you will have to lose to win. What's better, you must say to yourself, making love or creating frustration, although sometimes the making up is worth it. Mutual love is doing whatever you must to make your partner happy. This can only be done when we keep each other's best interests in mind through respect, honor, and consideration in all we do. Now, let's remember that this is not an overnight success story. It comes with time and a lot of work on both parts. Marriage is like a construction site, a work in progress. Let's keep working at it!!

Personal Reflection
God, what am I to learn from this nugget and scripture?

_____

_____

_____

_____

_____

_____

Day 53

Greet ye one another with a kiss of charity.
Peace be with you that are in Christ Jesus. Amen
I Peter 5:14(KJV)

Believe it or not, the simplest gestures that we extend to each other can mean so much to complete our day. To say that genuine love minds its manners means we won't step across each other and fail to say excuse me. When we do things for each other, a small word like thank you lets us know that what we did was appreciated and not taken for granted. Be a good listener and speak politely even when you're tired. Our spouse shouldn't have to bear the brunt of our bad day. Coming in contact with them should be refreshing, where we can refuel for another day. Congratulate each other on your successes and encourage one another when you fall short of a goal you set. Finally, know how to greet your spouse when you see them. Embrace them with a hug and kiss them, exchanging the juices that keep your love strong. This is also how you should release them into a new day.

Personal Reflection
What is this nugget saying to me, and how can I apply it in my marriage?

_____

_____

_____

_____

_____

Day 54

And the peace of God, which passeth all understanding,
shall keep your hearts and minds through Christ Jesus.
Philippians 4:7(KJV)

Your attitude will affect your altitude. How high do you want your marriage and your love life to peak? There may be times in your marriage that the both of you will require an attitude adjustment. Your attitudes will have much to do with the atmosphere you both set when you are around each other. To avoid friction in your relationship may mean that there will be times when you will have to do what is necessary for the peace of the environment. Nothing's worse than walking around each other with few words and a tense atmosphere. Practice resolving issues with compromise, respect, and consideration for each other. Again, it's an opportunity to set another kind of atmosphere. Know what I mean?

Personal Reflection
How can I apply this nugget to my marriage?

_____

_____

_____

_____

_____

_____

_____

Day 55

The steps of a good man are ordered by the Lord.
And He delights in his way.
Psalms 37:23(KJV)

To be gracious is to be respectful, courteous, and encouraging. When we do the opposite of these, we are faced with a nagging or insulting partner. We should do everything we can to avoid finding fault or being condescending to each other. Find ways to accentuate the positive. Highlight those things that they do right. Don't always emphasize their bad habits, not having a job, or their faults and failures. Always "edify". In the gospel song "Order My Steps", the writer's prayer to God is "bridle my tongue, let my words edify." We will find conversation and words to build each other as we learn to appreciate each other despite our shortcomings. I love you because . . .

Personal Reflection
How can this nugget help to transform my marital relationship?

_____

_____

_____

_____

_____

_____

Day 56

And as ye would men should do to you, do ye also to them likewise.
Luke 6:31(KJV)

Love is not selfish. It always considers the well-being and concern of others. If I love you, I will never do anything out of spite or with bad intentions. Be kind and courteous to your mate. You should treat your mate as you treat your God, with honor, love, and respect. Never treat others better than you treat the one you love. Treat them as if God has stamped on their foreheads, "Handle with care."

Personal Reflection
How has this nugget impacted and spoken to you today?

_____

_____

_____

_____

_____

_____

_____

Day 57

The words of a wise man's mouth are gracious;
but the lips of a fool will swallow up himself.
Ecclesiastes 10:12(KJV)

Words are precious. They can build up, or they can tear down. The Word of God says, "life and death are in the power of the tongue." Whatever you say to your mate should be spoken with caution so as not to offend or degrade. That's why practicing praising and complimenting each other is so important. This will lead to your mate showing great appreciation for you being their partner for life. The words from your mouth that cause displeasure and can leave scars because your words cut your spouse so profoundly. At this point, you need to take the time and make them right with words that can heal. Always be careful with what you say; you can't take it back once you've said it.

Personal Reflection
How does this nugget and scripture speak to me in the words I speak?

_____

_____

_____

_____

_____

_____

Day 58

God is our refuge and strength, a very present help in trouble.
Psalms 46:1(KJV)

When I reflect on our marriage, I see two lives that have blossomed into an extraordinary friendship, but not without its share of trouble. Marriage brought many bumps, turmoil, financial strains, and frustration. In our early years, we both had reservations about whether this would last. But the years together and loving each other amid those bad times had a favorable twist on us. If we could weigh the good and the bad times, we can say, as the songster Rev. Paul Jones, "when I look around and think things over, all our good days outweigh our bad days." We won't complain.

As you deal with the pressured times of your marriage, remember that you are in it to win it. This person is my soul mate for life. I will love them with all my heart and even more when times get tough. "So, when you're dealt lemons, just squeeze and make lemonade."

Personal Reflection
How can this nugget help me to realize the seriousness of marriage and appreciate all that comes with it?

_____

_____

_____

_____

Day 59

Therefore, humble yourselves under the mighty hand of God,
that He may exalt you in due time,
casting all your care upon Him, for He cares for you.
I Peter 5:6-7(NKJV)

Finding opportunities to create stress in your home or your marriage is never good. When those opportunities arise, it is always good to process the situation before opening your mouth. When your spouse has done something to irritate you, it might be a good time for you to calmly develop a way to express to them how their actions irritate you. If you are the irritator, you must find a way to say "I'm sorry" and lay out a plan of action for what you will do differently so this does not happen again. As time goes on, you will KNOW those things that irritate them. Love will help you find a way for you not to.

Personal Reflection
How can I apply the scripture and nugget to my marriage?

_____

_____

_____

_____

_____

_____

Day 60

For all have sinned, and come short of the glory of God.
Romans 3:23(NKJV)

We are often guilty of shifting blame and highlighting the faults and failures of others. Our best tool to use for passing judgment should be "self-evaluation." Remember that both of you came into the marriage with excess baggage. As we go through the sequence of marriage events with prayer and God's help, we can look at each other with another set of lenses and know that neither of us has arrived. We are still on the wheel of God, and He is pushing us toward purpose each day. Start accentuating the positive and refrain from negative finger-pointing. Know that God still loves us amid our "mess", so we must also learn to love our lovers for life with their shortcomings.

Personal Reflection
What can I learn from this nugget and scripture?

_____

_____

_____

_____

_____

_____

Day 61

He that is slow to anger is better than the mighty;
and he that ruleth his spirit than he that taketh a city.
Proverb 16:32(KJV)

One of the needed ingredients in a marriage is maintaining self-control. It is a way of bringing your emotions under control. You have a choice to be angry or not. Temperance allows us to PAUSE or STOP, reflect and choose the greater, remain calm, and seek spiritual guidance through the Holy Ghost.

THINK BEFORE YOU ACT!!

Personal Reflection
How can this nugget help me and improve who I am?

_____

_____

_____

_____

_____

_____

_____

Day 62

For if ye forgive men their trespasses,
your heavenly Father will also forgive you.
Matthew 6:14(KJV)

We should make it our business never to offend the one we love. When we react with our emotions, we sometimes say things that we cannot take back and may become offensive to our mate. When there are moments that you have contention or issues that need to be resolved, it is not good to attack your spouse without taking the time to think the matter over. The wisdom you need to deal with whatever is going on in your marriage can only come from the Holy Ghost. Try holding your marriage above all the issues that may arise. Also, remember that when the issue is resolved, walk in a spirit of forgiveness. Holding on to the problem and not having a forgiving spirit will hold your marriage in "bondage." Remember that we serve a forgiving God. When we can't forgive, how can He forgive us? Ask for His help and trust God to give you what you need to pass this hurdle and set you free. Whom the Lord sets free is free indeed.

Personal Reflection
God, what am I to learn from this nugget and scripture?

_____

_____

_____

_____

_____

Day 63

Cease from anger, and forsake wrath: fret not thyself in any wise to do evil.
Psalms 37:8(KJV)

Anger is a normal emotion we possess, and it sometimes can be healthy. It is also an emotion that we need to keep our eyes on. If it is not handled correctly, it can smother our love and affection for each other. Our marriages will depend on how we deal with anger. For some, it can turn to violence and an abusive relationship. We were meant to walk together and not to tread on the character and integrity of our mates. We should never let our anger tear each other down or resort to abuse verbally or physically. When you can't deal with anger, it is an excellent time to consult God for help. There will be times in your marriage when anger will rear its head; do this for me: (1) Don't let conflict and disagreements go unresolved, (2) Remember that you can't change your mate, only God can, and (3) Because you love each other, know when to end confrontation and seek God for wisdom.

Personal Reflection
How has this nugget today spoken to me and my marital relationship?

_____

_____

_____

_____

_____

_____

Day 64

Two are better than one; because they have a good reward for their labour.
For if they fall, the one will lift up his fellow:
but woe to him that is alone when he falleth;
for he hath no another to help him up.
Ecclesiastes 4:9-10(KJV)

The joy of love is making your partner happy. Love is not annoying or aggravating. When you are in love with your partner, you will enjoy each other's company and sharing moments. When you have found true love, you must do whatever it takes to hold on to it. It's a treasure.

"Marriage is not a ritual or an end. It is a long, intricate, intimate dance together, and nothing matters more than your sense of balance and your choice of partner."
- Amy Bloom

Personal Reflection
How can I apply the scripture and nugget to my marriage?

_____

_____

_____

_____

_____

_____

Day 65

Therefore, my beloved brethren,
be ye steadfast, unmoveable, always abounding in the work of the Lord,
forasmuch as ye know that your labour is not in vain in the Lord.
I Corinthians 15:58(KJV)

Marriage is a marathon. A marathon requires strength and endurance, as well as will your marriage. The marriage trail is long, and you will experience those who cheer you on and those who will not wish you well. Sometimes, you will experience periods of pain and disappointment, but you will find that the "good" will always outweigh the bad. In a marathon, you must have a mind to run the race with patience and perseverance; you will need that same mode of thinking for your marriage. Paul tells us about life's race. It's filled with many winds, turns, bumps, and bruises, but the joy is finishing the race till death do us part. He tells us that "the race is not given to the swift nor the strong, but to the one that endures till the end. Keep running the marriage race with a mind to "finish." Let nothing deter you from your faithfulness to your God and your marriage. Run on!!!!

Personal Reflection
God, what am I to learn from this nugget and scripture?

_____

_____

_____

_____

_____

Day 66

And when you stand praying, forgive, if ye have ought against any:
that your Father also which is in heaven may forgive you your trespasses.
Mark 11:25(KJV)

It isn't easy at times for us to deal with forgiveness. Our human behavior suggests that we find ways to retaliate and get even with the person who has hurt us. Our pride is injured, and our hopes and dreams for that person are somewhat tainted. Remember, not being able to forgive will hold you in bondage. Because love abides in our houses, we must strive to forgive when the opportunity presents itself. Remember that you, too, have flaws and shortcomings and that we are imperfect people. Think about the love God has for us; while we were yet sinners, stinking in sin, He loved us in spite of. Only God, through the Holy Spirit, can give us what we need to forgive.

Personal Reflection
How has this nugget impacted and spoken to you today?

_____

_____

_____

_____

_____

_____

Day 67

Thy Word is a lamp unto my feet and a light unto my path.
Psalms 119:105(KJV)

Marriage is sometimes filled with stress, but you can get through it. It is all a matter of diet. It is necessary that you eat what is appropriate for a healthy life spiritually and physically. The Word of God is good eating. The Bible says that it's not what goes in the mouth that defiles you but what comes out. If your diet consists of prayer and the Word of God, when stress rears its head, the words that come out of your mouth will speak to ANY situation you face. Hide the Word in your heart.

Personal Reflection
What am I to learn from this nugget and scripture today?

_____

_____

_____

_____

_____

_____

Day 68

Keep thy heart with all diligence; for out of it are the issues of life.
Proverbs 4:23(KJV)

The dictionary does not give meaning to your words, it's your heart. It is crucial to guard your heart and to do it with diligence. Protecting our hearts is part of our spiritual walk. It will help us discern outside forces detrimental to our lasting love for each other.

If you are guarding your heart, are you protecting your marriage? Know that the sanctity of marriage will always be under attack. It was first instituted by God. The enemy's job is to do all he can to destroy your love for each other through lies, doubt, unfaithfulness, and words of insult to each other, leading to divorce decisions. We will come into a marriage in love and think we are exempt from the toils and snares of a troubled marriage. Our marriages MUST be built on a solid base, and God himself is the source. When you make appliances that don't work correctly, the appropriate thing to do is to return them to the manufacturer. When things get shaky (your marriage), take it to the one (God) who designed it, and He will honor the warranty.

Personal Reflection
How is God speaking to me in this nugget today?

_____

_____

_____

_____

_____

_____

_____

_____

_____

_____

_____

Personal Reflection
What can I do to apply it to situations in my marriage?

_____

_____

_____

_____

_____

_____

_____

_____

_____

Day 69

What therefore God has joined together, let not man put asunder.
Mark 10:9(KJV)

Finding the source of a deep-seated issue in a marriage is often challenging. For couples, it's usually the product of a misunderstanding or something taken the wrong way by a spouse. It is always good to approach an angry situation calmly. There should be an agreement between both of you that you would refrain from attacking each other in anger. First, acknowledge that there is an issue and seek a calm resolution. Be sure of your love for each other. Because you love each other, there should never be moments of insecurity. Each day, demonstrate your love for each other by validating your spouse to remove all doubt that there are insecurities. If this is done, there should never be a time when you feel threatened by the invasive gestures of another. You know that you know who you are joined to for love. There should never be any doubt.

Personal Reflection
How can I apply this nugget and scripture to my marriage?

_____

_____

_____

_____

_____

_____

_____

_____

_____

_____

_____

Personal Reflection
What can I do to apply it to situations in my marriage?

_____

_____

_____

_____

_____

_____

_____

_____

_____

Day 70

Now the God of hope fill you with all joy and peace in believing,
that ye may abound in hope, through the power of the Holy Ghost.
Romans 15:13(KJV)

Love is an extraordinary sensation you experience when spending time with the one you care so deeply for. Love will make you remain committed to a person in making the relationship work, even in times when you don't feel so in love. It is the celebration of good and bad times. When you are in love, you desire your marriage to work, so you must work on it, nurture it, and help to grow it. One of the things that God gives us is the freedom of choice. So is the saving, building, and growing of your marriage. Love is like a bank account; you can only withdraw if you've made deposits. Every day should be a day with new deposits. Deposit trust, respect, encouragement, commitment, excitement, and intimacy. Whatever you put in is what you can withdraw. Make deposits daily. The dividends are great!

Personal Reflection
God, what am I to learn from this nugget and scripture?

_____

_____

_____

_____

_____

_____

Day 71

By this shall all men know that you are my disciples,
if ye have love one to another.
John 13:35(KJV)

One passage of scripture used in most wedding ceremonies is in Corinthians 13, Paul's interpretation of love is that it is full of action, experienced and demonstrated. He goes on to say that love is not envious and not displeased when others are experiencing success. Love and jealousy contradict each other. There's no way for you to love and be jealous of another. One of the most essential spiritual gifts we can have is the gift of love. All of the traits mentioned are descriptions of the actual essence of Jesus Christ. It is the perfect example of the agape love that should exist in our marriages. We can always celebrate the successes of our mate and others, but we must know that love is at the heart and soul of our relationship. Check yourself and see if your love is demonstrated in your marriage.

Personal Reflection
God, what am I to learn from this nugget and scripture?

_____

_____

_____

_____

_____

_____

Day 72

*This being so, I myself always strive to have a conscience
without offense toward God and men.*
Acts 24:16 (NKJV)

In marriage you should strive to make it your business to clear your conscience of all things that may be distracting or detrimental to your relationship. That means always keeping the lines of communication open and being able to share your faults and failures with your partner. Never try to hide things from your mate because it will jeopardize their trust in you.

Shakespeare had a famous quote, "To thine own self be true." Until we are first true to ourselves, can we be true to another. Truth will truly set us free; it is very vital to the healing process. We are then able to come to terms with our weaknesses and be strengthened by being open and honest. So, when you're in doubt as to your motives for not being truthful to your mate, take the time and do some soul-searching. Take a moment today and read Psalms 139. It will be an eye-opener for you and your relationship regarding God and others. The Psalmist ends this Psalms with a powerful request in verses 23-24.

Personal Reflection

How can I apply this nugget and scripture to help strengthen my marriage?

_____

_____

_____

_____

_____

Day 73

Many waters cannot quench love, neither can the floods drown it:
if a man would give all the substance of his house for love,
it would utterly be contemned.
Song of Solomon 8:6(KJV)

Love is a sense of becoming. It has not arrived, but it is a work in progress. We live with the hope that God will help us in what he designed the marriage to be. We were created not to talk love or think love, but to become love. Christ is the best example of someone who exemplifies love to its fullest. There is a quote by an unknown author that says, "Meeting you was fate, becoming your friend was a choice, but falling in love with you was beyond my control." Love isn't about becoming somebody else's perfect person because we are imperfect people, it's about finding someone who helps you become the best person you can be.

Personal Reflection
What can I gain from this scripture and nugget today?

_____

_____

_____

_____

_____

_____

_____

Day 74

There are three things which are too wonderful for me, yea, four which I know not: the way of an eagle; the way of a serpent upon a rock; the way of a ship in the midst of the sea; and the way of a man with a maid.
Proverbs 30:18-19(KJV)

When we look at marriage, we see two lives merging. The Bible says that the two-flesh become one. That means a synergy takes place; two people with different personalities, belief systems, and life patterns merge into one. We take each other's baggage and must learn that we come into the relationships with many unknowns.

No marriage is perfect; there is no perfect union. Problems will arise, but we solemnly vow to love, honor, and cherish each other until death. That means accepting my partner with everything they bring to the marriage, knowing with God's help our love will result in the most unity, love, and fulfillment we could have. This synergy is equivalent to God's "agape" love for us. He loves us despite. We must love our partner lovingly even when facing life's challenges by exhibiting patience, kindness, and understanding. Your love for each other will help to validate your marriage. In essence, you will bring out the best in each other.

Personal Reflection
How does this nugget and scriptural passage speak to me about God's design for marriage?

_____

_____

_____

_____

_____

Day 75

Therefore, shall a man leave his father and mother,
and shall cleave unto his wife: and they shall be one flesh
Genesis 2:24(KJV)

In this marriage journey, we will both discover that our mate is full of purpose and potential. Knowing that God is a God of purpose, He will show us that we are both pregnant with unlimited possibilities that will help us to be what he has purposed us to be, which includes our lives together. Knowing that each of us bring gifts and talents to the marriage will help us discover those things that make us complete. When God said, "It is not good for man to be alone," he knew we were not complete without a helpmate. This means that something was lacking or a deficiency. He then provided each of us with what was missing. Together, we form a union to make a perfect match. So today, take the opportunity to explore and recognize what each of you bring to the marriage.

Personal Reflection
God, what am I to learn from this nugget and scripture?

_____

_____

_____

_____

_____

_____

Day 76

Death and life are in the power of the tongue:
and they that love it shall eat of the fruit thereof.
Proverbs 18:21(KJV)

Honor your partner often for being your partner, for choosing you to be their lover for life. We all need a positive perspective to have a healthy and nurturing relationship. Having that positive attitude helps to diminish times of stress and helps to create an atmosphere of love and respect for each other. There should always be a desire to believe that there is some good in each of us. Never lend your marriage to misery and negativity.

We should also recognize that we have the power to "shift" the atmosphere. We do that by accentuating the positive and eliminating the negative. Even when your partner messes up, we can still "choose" to believe that there is good in our spouse. Speak what you know to be true about your spouse. My husband is loving; my wife is supportive. Your marriage will be what you speak. Speak positive!

Personal Reflection
How can this nugget and scripture be applied to my marriage?

_____

_____

_____

_____

_____

Day 77

Finally, brethren, whatsoever things are true,
whatsoever things are honest, whatsoever things are just, whatsoever things are pure,
whatsoever things are lovely, whatsoever things are of good report;
if there be any virtue, and if there be any praise, think on these things.
Philippians 4:8(KJV)

Knowing that you are being appreciated by your spouse is always encouraging. We all want that validation that our partner sees us, that they recognize what we do daily and yet appreciate our every effort. It's not good to be bombarded with the hustle of our everyday regiment that we miss out on little opportunities to connect as a couple.

Proverbs tells us how a virtuous woman gains the praise of those around her who appreciate her. Her children arise and call her blessed; her husband also praises her (Proverbs 31:28). Take the time to show how much you appreciate each other. Sometimes it's good to hear the words, "I appreciate you."

Personal Reflection
How can this scripture and nugget help me to appreciate my spouse better?

_____

_____

_____

_____

_____

Day 78

And let us not be weary in well doing:
for in due season we shall reap, if we faint not.
Galatians 6:9(KJV)

Love is not jealous: Jealousy is a disease that can plague like cancer and create a barrier in your marriage. It prevents you from celebrating the successes of your partner. I am thrilled when my partner is recognized for their accomplishments because it reflects our oneness. Our success is a product of our encouragement to each other and just being a support system in whatever we undertake.

Jealousy is just insecurity in a mask. Recognize when it is not your season, and rejoice when others celebrate theirs. If you just hold on, your day will come in "due" season. Be confident in who you are and rejoice in the accomplishments and successes of your partner and those around you.

Personal Reflection
What can I use in this nugget to help move our marriage in a positive direction?

_____

_____

_____

_____

_____

_____

Day 79

No temptation has overtaken you except such as is common to man;
but God is faithful, who will not allow you to be tempted beyond what you are able,
but with the temptation will also make a way to escape,
that you may be able to bear it.
I Corinthians 10:13(NKJV)

Jealousy can be perceived as a threat to your partner, which can be the fatal blow to terminating your marriage. It is hard to shake because it cuts at the core of your emotions. If it exists in your marriage, it will keep your marriage under the bondage of frustration and damage your relationship. This has to be a soul-searching process, first by acknowledging your jealous behavior. Share it with your partner and seek the needed help to rid yourself of this poisonous "spirit." Save your marriage by giving this problem to God and asking him to free you of this spirit of jealousy. You must first recognize who you are in Christ and re-evaluate your walk with him.

Personal Reflection
What can I learn from this nugget and scripture?

_____

_____

_____

_____

_____

_____

Day 80

Again, I say unto you, that if two of you shall agree on earth concerning anything that they ask, it will be done for them by my Father in heaven.
Matthew 18:19(NKJV)

I am proud that I am married to someone who has been my greatest supporter and number one fan for all the years we have been together. Whatever my undertakings, they have been there to cheer, support, assist, and participate in my successes. There will never be room for envy when we learn to be that support system and encourager in our marriages. We must celebrate each other every chance we get. In marriage, we lean and depend on each other; when my partner is experiencing success, I am thrilled because I know that I am a part of whatever success they are experiencing. A good suggestion would be to spend more time with each other and open your heart to each other. Ask the essential questions: What can I do to help you with this or that. How can I better support you? Love is not selfish. It's not about us individually, but what WE can do TOGETHER.

Personal Reflection
How does this nugget speak to me and my relationship with my spouse?

_____

_____

_____

_____

_____

_____

Day 81

And He said unto me, My grace is sufficient for thee:
for my strength is made perfect in weakness.
Most gladly therefore will I rather glory in my infirmities,
that the power of Christ may rest upon me.
II Corinthians 12:9 (NKJV)

I am fascinated by the statement, "You complete me." Again, I had to go back to God's original intent for the creation of Eve for Adam and vice versa. God took a part of man to form him a partner; nothing was deficient about her. She was just like her mate, with some exceptions. They were designed to complement each other in more ways than the physical. Whatever I'm lacking, my partner makes up the difference. There are some things my spouse may be better at or handle better than I can. It doesn't make me any less of a partner, but it helps me acknowledge their gifts and how they enhance our marriage and relationship.

Personal Reflection

How can I best apply the concept of the giftings that we both bring to the marriage?

_____

_____

_____

_____

_____

_____

Day 82

Therefore, I take pleasure in infirmities, in reproaches,
in necessities, in persecution,
in distresses for Christ's sake: for when I am weak, then am I strong.
II Corinthians 12:10(NKJV)

Because we are one, we are a team working towards the same goal, trying to achieve what the Lord has placed before us. We should acknowledge the shortcomings of both of us. When I am weak, feeling down, disappointed, and hurt, my spouse is the one who lifts me up. There shouldn't be anyone else you can trust with your heart other than your spouse. Celebrate each other.

Personal Reflection
What can I learn from this nugget and scripture?

_____

_____

_____

_____

_____

_____

_____

Day 83

Withhold not good from them to whom it is due,
when it is in the power of thine hand to do it.
Proverbs 3:27 (KJV)

Men appreciate their wives standing behind them, pushing them to "become." Become what God has purposed them to be as husband, Father, provider, priest, and protector. We need your accolades and praises when we have done something worth your compliments. Never let that cheering come from another. It needs to come from you! We get praise and thanks from those in our churches, on our jobs, or in our communities, but the most incredible feeling in the world is to hear it from the mouth of the one who loves you. Invest in a cheerleading uniform, and in your private time, cheer your man on! I see a big explosion!! Booooom!!!

Personal Reflection
How can this nugget help me to better appreciate my spouse?

_____

_____

_____

_____

_____

_____

Day 84

But the fruit of the Spirit is love, joy, peace, longsuffering, gentleness, goodness, faith, meekness, temperance: against such there is no law.
Galatians 5:22 -23(NKJV)

Commit to being lifetime lovers, not lovers for the moment. Therefore, remember it is time to let love, humility, and gratefulness destroy any jealousy in your heart. It's time to let your mate's successes draw you closer together and give you greater opportunities to show genuine love. Showing your spouse love is not a once-in-while thing, but it's constant, repetitive, and never gets old. Lift each other up privately and publicly to affirm your love for one another. Renew your commitment every chance you get. Jeffrey Osborne says it this way:

Compliment what she does, send her roses just because
If it's violins she loves, let them play
Dedicate her favorite song and hold her closer all night long
Maybe she has it in her mine that she's just wasting her time
Love her today, find one hundred ways.

Personal Reflection

What am I to learn from this nugget and scripture as I seek to edify my spouse?

_____

_____

_____

_____

Day 85

Humble yourselves therefore under the mighty hand of God,
that he may exalt you in due time.
I Peter 5:6 (NKJV)

Resolve that you will take every opportunity you can to celebrate the relationship you have with your partner. Take the time to express your gratitude to each other. Renew your commitment every chance you get. Celebrate each other not just because it's a special day but any day. Validating your spouse is essential.

Personal Reflection

What can I learn from this nugget and scripture to help me in my marriage?

_____

_____

_____

_____

_____

_____

_____

_____

Day 86

Rejoice with those who rejoice; mourn with those who mourn.
Romans 12:15(NIV)

One of the characteristics of a true Christian is the ability to rejoice in the success of others. Many cannot rejoice with others. Instead, they look to tear down anything built by reacting with jealousy. Throughout the Bible, there are many calls to rejoice and celebrate. This is especially true because of God's original intent for marriage. Every minute of your marriage will not always be a bed of roses; there will be bumps and bruises. Proverbs is full of exhortations for couples to enjoy their relationships. When things aren't going as well as expected, we must still rejoice in our love for each other. Know that your "down" time is not permanent but temporary. Rejoice in knowing that "joy" will come in the morning.

Personal Reflection
God, what am I to learn from this nugget and scripture?

_____

_____

_____

_____

_____

_____

Day 87

Greet one another with a kiss of love.
1 Peter 5:14(NIV)

Kissing is showing affection to the one you love with your lips. Kisses have positive connotations like friendship, romance, and love. For me, it symbolizes how our love has unified all our years together. Kissing seals the love when you transfer a needed hormone to the other. Make a habit of waking each morning with a kiss when leaving for work and your safe return home after a hard day. Kiss often and long! There are some excellent benefits.

Personal Reflection

What can I learn from this nugget and scripture to help me show affection better?

_____

_____

_____

_____

_____

_____

_____

Day 88

Let your light so shine before men that they may see your good works,
and glorify your father which is in heaven.
Matthew 5:16 (NKJV)

Love is demonstrated in our actions. It affects your emotions, facial expressions, verbal expression, and temperance. Love cannot be hidden or disguised by pretenses. How you act and respond to your spouse indicates your love for each other. That's why validating your love for one another daily is so important. Because your love runs deep, there won't be opportunities for others to see periods when love is absent. Don't allow what God has ordained and put together to dwindle and resort to a dull, unfulfilled relationship that simply exists in name only. Someone is watching you. Let your marriage speak life and love powered by God.

Personal Reflection
How does this nugget and scripture speak to me and my marriage?

_____

_____

_____

_____

_____

_____

Day 89

I am my beloved's, and my beloved is mine: he feedeth among the lilies.
Song of Solomon 6:3(KJV)

I'm a firm believer that how you start, you will finish. One of the most precious moments in marriage is a salutation from the one you love. I can receive it from a host of friends and acquaintances, but there's something special about a greeting sealed with a kiss from my lover. When I've had a rough day at work and even a challenge among the saints, it is a great feeling to be greeted by the one who eases the tension and shifts my atmosphere. Make it your business to start your morning and seal your day with sweet salutations to each other. It will be medicine to your relationship and your marriage. Remember to love hard!

Personal Reflection
How can I better demonstrate love to my spouse?

_____

_____

_____

_____

_____

_____

_____

Day 90

The discretion of a man deterreth his anger;
and it is his glory to pass over a transgression.
Proverbs 19:11(KJV)

Think back to the story Jesus told of the prodigal son. Of all the scenarios this young man had played in his mind, this was likely the last one he expected. But how do you think it made him feel to receive his father's embrace and hear his thankful tone? He no doubt felt loved and treasured once again. What do you think it did to their relationship? What kind of greetings would make your mate feel like this? (See Luke 15:11-32) This is the same feeling you get when we have fallen short of something during our marriage. There will be times when we may not be pleased with the actions of our partners, but the joy of it all is that we can look past our mistakes and have a heart of compassion and forgiveness. We realize the circle can never be complete when we have not dealt with the issues that caused us distress.

Emulate the father of the prodigal son, love beyond the faults and failures, and restore your unconditional love for each other. Remember also that unforgiveness will hinder your prayer life. If God can look beyond our flaws, we must be willing to love despite them. Love covers a multitude of faults.

Personal Reflection
God, what am I to learn from this nugget and scripture?

_____

_____

_____

_____

_____

_____

_____

_____

_____

Personal Reflection
How can I apply it to my marriage?

_____

_____

_____

_____

_____

_____

_____

_____

Day 91

Be ye followers of me, even as I also am of Christ.
I Corinthians 11:1 (KJV)

Love always makes a good impression on the person we love. When we choose to love someone, we are always mindful of our actions. How we talk to and treat them should always be in our minds. When our love makes a good impression, you will never see or experience periods of tearing down but edification. There should never be any doubt as to our love for each other. Our love for our spouse should be like a billboard, and everyone will see evidence of our love for each other. As Matthew mentions in chapter five, verse fourteen, our love is set upon a hill that cannot be hidden. What kind of impressions are you making with your marriage?

Personal Reflection

How can I make this nugget and passage applicable to our marriage?

_____

_____

_____

_____

_____

_____

_____

Day 92

And we know that all things work together for good to them that love God,
to them who are the called according to His purpose.
Romans 8:28 (KJV)

How do you make your spouse feel? Does your spouse feel valued and appreciated? Do they feel loved? Even when you're not getting along, you can lessen the tension and give them value by how you greet them.

Personal Reflection
How can my demonstration of love help to shape my marriage?

_____

_____

_____

_____

_____

_____

_____

_____

Day 93

But if any provide not for his own, and especially those of his own house,
he hath denied the faith, and is worse than an infidel.
I Timothy 5:8 (KJV)

When we talk about value, we think about the usefulness or importance of a thing. One of my most valued possessions is the woman that I married. Besides having a relationship with God, your spouse should be your most valuable treasure. How can I value them? It is crucial for me first to make them feel valued and not just a convenient part of your relationship. They should be second only to God, not even your church. Understand that God created the family first! Love your spouse hard and work toward them being your lifetime lover.

Personal Reflection
How can I reflect on today's nugget and scripture? What is it saying to me?

_____

_____

_____

_____

_____

_____

_____

Day 94

Except the Lord build the house, they labour in vain that build it:
except the Lord keep the city the watchman waketh in vain.
Psalms 127:1 (KJV)

Is it possible to fall out of love, or were you ever in love? Do we fall out of love because of some mishap or the mistake of a mate, or because we refuse to put the time in to make it work? Love is not built on a condition. I love you because of what you can do for me and not what we can do "together." We often marry for the physical or the material, but unlike our spiritual journey, these things will not last.

Marriage is a work, a covenant between the two of you. It is a period when you learn to appreciate each other's differences and cope with knowing that you are not perfect and are in the process of "becoming." Remember that the grass may seem greener on the other side because you see other marriages a little better than yours. Know that they didn't get there overnight. It was a process by which "both" of them had to work. Take a little time and read the first few chapters of Hosea. It will be a refresher for you.

Personal Reflection

How does the nugget and scripture help me to reflect on my marriage?

_____

_____

_____

_____

_____

_____

Day 95

Many waters cannot quench love; rivers cannot sweep it away.
If one were to give all the wealth of his house for love, it would be utterly scorned.
Song of Solomon 8:7(NIV)

Loving unconditionally is a challenging task. It can only be accomplished with the help of God. Can you love me with all my faults, flaws, and failures? Can you look beyond the "mess" and still find it in your heart to love your mate unconditionally? That means loving without conditions. This kind of love means loving your partner no matter what. You are no longer the center of your world. They are. Love is unconditional when it endures all things, overcomes them, and survives them all.

Personal Reflection
God, what am I to learn from this nugget and scripture?

_____

_____

_____

_____

_____

_____

_____

Day 96

And over all these virtues put on love,
which binds them all together in perfect unity.
Colossians 3:14 (NIV)

These are familiar words that we vowed on the day we stood before God and a company of people to declare our love for each other. It meant that we were committed to each other despite whatever we go through, our downfalls and mishaps, and we will survive it together.

There are primary conditions necessary for any relationship to be healthy and safe. They are mutual caring, mutual honesty, and mutual respect. The word that leaps out at me is mutual. One person can certainly make a good relationship bad all by themselves, but one person cannot turn a bad relationship into a good relationship all by themselves. It will take both of you working together with a mutual understanding to make your relationship good. Vow to go all the way, through the thick and the thin, loving each other unconditionally.

Personal Reflection
God, what am I to learn from this nugget and scripture?

_____

_____

_____

_____

_____

_____

_____

Day 97

For God so loved the world that He gave His only begotten Son,
that whosoever believeth in Him should not perish, but have everlasting life.
John 3:16 (NJV)

This is an example of the true love of Jesus. He took on the world's sins and bore them on the cross because of his genuine love for us. He could've come down, but yet he endured the pain and the shame just for us all. This was done because God told him to do it. How many of us would make that sacrifice for our mate? God told man to take on a wife and love her unconditionally, and the wife should love her husband in the same manner. However, when things become unbearable, rough, and challenging and begin to look bleak in our marriages, we make choices unlike those that Jesus made. He could have saved himself, but he stayed upon the cross and allowed them to drive stakes in his hands and feet. He allowed them to pierce him in his side. Now that's love. We may not go to the extreme that Jesus went to save the world, but within our marriages, we need to develop an enduring love that will endure all things.

Personal Reflection
How has this nugget and scripture spoken to me as I emulate the ways of Christ?

_____

_____

_____

_____

_____

Day 98

Love your spouse hard and work toward them being your lifetime lover.
Wives, submit yourselves to your own husbands as you do the Lord.
Ephesians 5:22 (NIV)

Spend time this week making your spouse feel valued and special. Begin with spending quality time in conversation, intimacy, and enjoying each other's company. You know the mind and heart of your Creator because you spend time in fellowship with Him. The same is required when you love your spouse. Love for our spouse is something we learn fresh and new each day. When done the right way, it will become exciting and renewed. We never can say this enough.

Personal Reflection
What am I to gain from this nugget and scripture?

_____

_____

_____

_____

_____

_____

_____

Day 99

*And we have known and believed the love that God hath to us, God is love;
and he that dwelleth in love dwelleth in God, and God in him.*
I John 4:16(KJV)

Marriage is not something that happens to us. We chose to get married, and our marriage was created to where it is now as our love grew. That means how I behave in my marriage and how I treat my wife (or husband) profoundly affects my marriage. This simple statement has profound implications because how you treat your spouse, lover, and soulmate can positively or negatively impact your marriage and its duration. Read Ephesians 5:25-33 because it tells a husband how to love his wife just as Christ loves the church. In the same way, husbands ought to love their wives as they love their own bodies. A man who loves his wife shows love for himself. He cares for his body by feeding and caring for it, just as Christ cares for the church.

Through your unwavering committed love, you and your spouse should learn how to live each day with unbridled exuberance and joy, seizing every moment and following your heart. Learn to appreciate the simple things in life that cost you nothing. Learn to be optimistic in the face of adversity. Maintain a friendship, selflessness, and unwavering loyalty to your love for one another.

Personal Reflection
God, what am I to learn from this nugget and scripture?

_____

_____

_____

_____

_____

_____

_____

_____

_____

_____

_____

Personal Reflection
How has this nugget impacted and spoken to you today?

_____

_____

_____

_____

_____

_____

_____

Day 100

It (love) always protects, always trust, always hopes, always perseveres.
I Corinthians 13: 7(NIV)

It's not strange that God, the essence of love, intended for love to be the glue that holds it together. When man was alone, it was the missing ingredient. God filled the void after seeing that everything created was good, and love entered the scene.

It transcends all the blemishes, struggles, and difficult times you may face in your marriage. You will encounter some tough times when you have invested time in a marriage for any period. But God's kind of love covers a multitude of faults. It is equivalent to Jesus' love for us; that while we were yet sinners, he died for us. So, when God looks at us, he sees us "covered." There may be seasons when you want to act in anger, but you choose to operate in love. The love we should have for each other helps the other walk in a way worthy of that love. Love is not just an expression but an act.

Personal Reflection
How can I apply this passage of scripture and nugget to my marriage?

_____

_____

_____

_____

_____

Day 101

But they that wait upon the Lord shall renew their strength; they shall mount up with wings as eagles; they shall run, and not be weary; and they shall walk, and not faint.
Isaiah 40:31(KJV)

There is a lot to learn in a marriage, but we must realize it takes time to build our marriage into a successful one. Learning how to organize our union and not expecting it to work itself is where we begin. It's how we work to empower our relationship. An empowered relationship exists with a level of purpose and does not coast on autopilot. We have to embrace the phases that our marriages may experience. Many of us do our marital journey a disservice because we expect it to live forever in a particular stage. Subsequently, this is because we are creatures of habit who get comfortable with the familiar.

Whether it is the stage of romance and frequent sex, building our nest with children and their activities, or building our careers and financial security, we have to accept that each stage can impact our relationship negatively or positively.

Personal Reflection
What must I do in my marriage to remain positive when our relationship experiences another phase change?

_____

_____

_____

_____

_____

Day 102

Many are the woes of the wicked,
but the Lord's unfailing love surrounds the one who trusts in him.
Psalm 32:10(NIV)

No marriage can survive without trust. It is something that is cultivated and nurtured by each of you. If you aren't actively working to build trust, you will find that your relationship will be full of holes that the enemy will quickly penetrate, and the outcome is disaster. One key factor in trust is never allowing issues in your marriage to go unresolved. Handle them with care.

The writer of Proverbs says, "trust in the Lord with all thine heart and lean not to thine own understanding." Trust is as essential to your marriage as faith is to your walk with God. So, in your marriage, trust your partner and acknowledge your trust in them. The key is NEVER to give your mate a reason not to trust you. Trust is one of the main ingredients in a marriage; without love and trust, a marriage will not work.

Personal Reflection

How can I demonstrate trust so that my spouse will never have reason for doubt?

_____

_____

_____

_____

_____

_____

Day 103

In this same way, husbands ought to love their wives as their own bodies.
He who loves his wife loves himself.
Psalms 32:10(NIV)

For this cause shall a man leave his father and mother and shall be joined unto his wife, and they two shall be one flesh". The wife is part of your body; therefore, you are part of each other. When a man gives his daughter away during the wedding ceremony, he gives her to her husband in hopes that he will love her as he loves himself. She bears his name, and if your name means anything to you, you will strive to protect it by protecting your mate. Cherish the love of your life as if she is your prize possession. Honor her because she gave up her name for yours. Never subject her to ridicule, but protect her honor and your name. It's all about the love. Does your spouse know that you love her? How do you know? So, my brothers, "Love your wife, as Christ loved the church and gave himself for her."

Personal Reflection
How is my love demonstrated to my lover for life each day?

_____

_____

_____

_____

_____

_____

Day 104

Let all bitterness, and wrath, and anger, and clamour, and evil speaking, be put away from you, with all malice: And be ye kind one to another, tenderhearted, forgiving one another, even as God for Christ's sake hath forgiven you.
Ephesians 4:31-32(KJV)

Sometimes, when we get frustrated with our spouse for something they did or didn't do, we still need to be careful of our reaction. What if you could hear everything that you said to your spouse through their ears? If you could, would you keep talking like everything was okay and nothing had changed? Or would you stop talking now and then because you felt the pain of your words like your spouse?

Personal Reflection
What do I need to work on to communicate with my spouse compassionately?

_____

_____

_____

_____

_____

_____

_____

_____

_____

_____

_____

_____

Personal Reflection
How can I apply this passage of scripture and nugget to my marriage?

_____

_____

_____

_____

_____

_____

_____

_____

_____

Day 105

Let your speech always be with grace, seasoned with salt,
that you may know how you ought to answer each one.
Colossians 4:6(NKJV)

Sometimes, we glaze into our spouse's face during a tense discussion and see the pain from the words we chose to say. Does that look help you know the importance of carefully seasoning your words before you speak to them? You now know that your comments would affect you like they affected your spouse. I know sometimes you come home from work tired, frustrated, and exhausted regarding your day. However, your spouse was not on your job. Don't let your day dictate the tone you use with your spouse. You control that narrative.

Personal Reflection
What can I do to work on learning to speak lovingly during turmoil?

_____

_____

_____

_____

_____

_____

_____

Day 106

No weapon formed against you shall prosper, and every tongue which rises against you in judgment You shall condemn. This is the heritage of the servants of the Lord, and their righteousness is from Me, "Says the Lord."
Isaiah 54:17(NKJV)

When God created the family, we became the target of Satan. Satan's desire and intent has been to destroy marriage, family, and our love for God. When you said "I do", you and your marriage became a bull's eye. Anything the enemy can put before us to interfere with our love for each other is his primary attempt to kill, steal, and destroy our marriages. When faced with struggles, disappointments, chaos, and periods of separation, know that the enemy is forever at work. You must do all you can to preserve your love for each other by praying for your marriage and covering your mate. When love is shared and nurtured, the devil in hell can't penetrate it. His weapons may be formed against your marriage, but THEY WON'T WORK! Vow, as Paul, to let nothing separate you from your love for each other. Love plus Prayer equals A marriage that will survive the best and worst times.

Personal Reflection
How can I apply this passage of scripture and nugget to my marriage?

_____

_____

_____

_____

_____

_____

Day 107

Together, you can accomplish anything you dream of. Do everything in love.
1 Corinthians 16:14(NIV)

There's no harm in going all out for your mate. Because they are your soul mate, you must do the unthinkable for your lover. There is no limit to how you express your love at any cost. Our love is expressed on birthdays, anniversaries, Valentine's Day, and many other special days, but we take the time every day to go out of our way to show love. The Word says we should love our wives as Jesus loves the church. That means I'm sold out and dedicated to loving my partner. We must be willing to go out for things for our partner as we are to the important things to us. Be sensitive to your mate's needs, realize that you are in this thing together, and be thankful that you have a love that God has special ordered for you.

Personal Reflection
How can I apply this passage of scripture and nugget to my marriage?

_____

_____

_____

_____

_____

_____

_____

Day 108

Therefore, shall a man leave his father and his mother,
and shall cleave unto his wife: and they shall be one flesh.
Genesis 2:24(KJV)

Never compare your relationship to another. Every marriage is different and brings with it its share of problems. What looks good on the surface can be deceiving. There is no perfect marriage, and comparing your marriage to another may lead to resenting your mate. Look at what you have as a couple, and be thankful for who the Lord has blessed you with. Know that the love you have for each other is unique and special. Each day, God is leading our relationship to what he has purposed it to be. Our marriage is a work in process.

Personal Reflection

How can I work each day to make our marriage work for us?

_____

_____

_____

_____

_____

_____

_____

Day 109

In this same way, husbands ought to love their wives as their own bodies.
He who loves his wife loves himself.
Ephesians 5:28(NIV)

When you look into your lover's eyes, you should see a mirror image of yourself. MY VERY BEING REFLECTS YOU because I love you the way I do. I find energy each time I see you smile. It is good to know you are a vital part of me. Each day with you is special because with you, "I'm born again."

Personal Reflection
What am I doing in my marriage to reflect my love for my spouse?

_____

_____

_____

_____

_____

_____

_____

_____

Day 110

*Give, and it will be given to you: good measure, pressed down,
shaken together, and running over will be put into your bosom.
Luke 6:36 (NKJV)*

Do you see your spouse as an investment? When I look at an investment, I know that it is something I watch grow, close, and at a distance. Anything you invest in is something of quality that you intend to receive dividends. Those dividends are our endless love for each other and those precious moments spent learning about my partner's likes and dislikes. It is the ability to see the fruits of our labor of love evident in everything about our marriage. It does not need to be broadcasted, but it is evident in everything about us. Your investment will determine your return. How much are you investing? This is not a one-time deposit but a daily one. It includes my time, my ability to listen to my mate, and just being there after a tough day on the job or a significant disappointment. There may be moments when you feel like it's not worth it, but it will pay off in the long run. You get out of it what you put in it! How bad do you want it? Remember that this is a PARTNERSHIP!

Personal Reflection
What am I investing to give my marriage the greatest chance for survival?

_____

_____

_____

_____

_____

Day 111

Not looking to your own interests
but each of you to the interests of the others.
Philippians 2:4(NIV)

One of the attributes of Christ was that everywhere His feet trod, His mission was to make a difference. Our goal as the ministry of marriage is to each one, reach one and teach one. All you've learned through your experiences in marriage is not to be held to yourself but shared with other couples, especially our young people. Your assignment today is to share a nugget, even a past one, with a couple who you feel would appreciate an encouraging word. I'm sure that all of us at one time have experienced the distress calls of couples that may be struggling with their marriages. Never give advice, but offer your prayers and encouragement to them. A good word goes further than what we may deem as good advice.

Personal Reflection
Can others see the beauty of marriage in our walk and talk? How?

_____

_____

_____

_____

_____

_____

_____

Day 112

If we can first learn to submit to God, submitting to each other is easy.
Let us therefore follow after the things which make for peace,
and things wherewith one may edify another.
Romans 14:19(KJV)

Being in love with someone means wanting the best for them and always looking out for your partner's best interest. I submit to my mate because I have the mind of Christ in that He laid down His life for the good of humankind. Whatever I desire for myself, I share that same desire for my mate. They represent the epitome of love: unselfish, caring, humble, and gentle. As a wife and husband, we complement each other, especially our roles in the family. We are joint heirs to every blessing God has for our marriage union.

Personal Reflection
How well am I doing in submitting to my spouse? Are we complimenting each other?

_____

_____

_____

_____

_____

_____

Day 113

In your relationships with one another, have the same mindset as Christ Jesus.
Philippians 2:5(NIV)

One of the major issues in marriage is being able to resolve conflict. Can we disagree, and it doesn't end in periods of silence or pouting? This is unhealthy and may lead to other things that can harm your communication. You must know that this is inevitable in ALL marriages, but it doesn't mean you can't get through it. Remember that your marriage is a work in process and takes work. Disagreeing is nothing but a difference of opinion.

Both of you having an opinion makes you who you are, and it's healthy. How you resolve your disagreements is very important as well. Marriage is give and take. When you feel that this conflict is affecting your relationship, PRAY. Someone has to be the one to set the stage for God to do a "quick" work of bringing both of you back on one accord. You've got to believe that with God's power, it can be resolved when BOTH of you work at it.

Personal Reflection

How can I apply this passage of scripture and nugget to my marriage when there is conflict?

_____

_____

_____

_____

_____

_____

Day 114

But the wisdom that comes from heaven is first of all pure; then peace-loving, considerate, submissive, full of mercy and good fruit, impartial and sincere. (James 3:17(NIV)

The Bible says, " the fear of God is the beginning of wisdom." That means acknowledging and referencing God is the first thing we should always do. Nothing that we do as a couple will come without consulting God. Some think that there are some things that we won't need to consult God on, but the Word says, "in all thy ways acknowledge God, and He will direct your path." Who else can you get the best direction and guidance from? When we don't consult God, we make "fleshy" decisions that may jeopardize our relationships. It could result in unwanted debt, bad family decisions, a breakdown in communication, and a sour marriage. Before you decide on ANYTHING, consult God.

Personal Reflection
How are we seeking God in our goals and decision-making? Are we seeking His wisdom?

_____

_____

_____

_____

_____

_____

Day 115

Can two walk together, unless they be agreed?
Amos 3:3(KJV)

The secret in partnership or marriage is being able to value the opinions of each other. We come into the relationship as two people with different backgrounds or experiences. When we don't respect each other's views, we destroy our ability to be who we are. As time passes and your hearts and minds begin to gel, you will find it easy to hear things from another perspective. Our marriages will be successful when we can be individuals first and learn to accept each other with all our qualities and flaws.

Learning never stops!! You will be amazed at what we can learn from each other. I can share what my experiences have taught me and vice versa. It is crucial to gaining the respect we should have for each other. Learn first to LISTEN!!!

Personal Reflection
How am I valuing the opinions and perspectives of my spouse?

_____

_____

_____

_____

_____

_____

Day 116

When pride comes, then comes disgrace, but with humility comes wisdom.
Proverbs 11:2 (NIV)

Pride can be a dangerous thing. You will eventually suffer a setback or major disappointment when you have too much pride. It can damage your friendship relationship with your spouse and destroy your marriage. It's the thing that will make you feel offended when your mate gives constructive criticism to you. Criticism is a stepping stone to wisdom. Proverbs 23:11-12 says, "To one who listens, valid criticism is a gold earring or as an ornament. To save our relationships, take the time to examine yourself and take on a posture of humility. God has given us the freedom to choose. You can decide to rid yourself of pride so that you will not miss the blessings he has already prepared for you and yours. For the sake of the one you love, if this is an area of development for you, seek the wisdom of God that he will remove it and clothe you with a spirit of humbleness. Your marriage is well worth it!!

Personal Reflection
How can I apply this passage of scripture and nugget to my marriage?

_____

_____

_____

_____

_____

_____

Day 117

If it is possible, as far as it depends on you, live at peace with everyone.
Romans 12:18(NIV)

One of the most important things to me in marriage is maintaining "peace" in my home. Where there is no peace, there is stress, non-verbal communication, and contention. Home is where the heart is, where I long to be after a stress-filled day. We should have a spouse who provides the peace that can relax us and take our minds off what we've experienced in our day. Having peace in the home is a work in progress. Is it attainable? Yes. It's always good to seek God's assistance when it seems to be in turmoil. The Word of God says he can give us peace that passes all understanding. If he can calm a raging sea by saying, "peace be still, " he can speak peace to your mind and marriage.

Personal Reflection
How am I seeking peace in my home and my marriage?

_____

_____

_____

_____

_____

_____

Day 118

A gentle answer turns away wrath, but a harsh word stirs up anger.
Proverbs 15:1(NIV)

Do you know how to fight fair in your marriage? We are often not cautious of what we say to each other, which may lead to bitterness and communication breakdown. It would be best if you took the opportunity to think and choose your words carefully when there is contention among you. Remember, when it's said, you can't take it back. Will you become so angry that you say things that will destroy your relationship and sometimes damage the self-worth of your mate?

Sometimes, it may take you to take a TV "time out" where you can best filter what has been said and come back with something that may cause both of you to think about what is happening. This is the best time to use your listening skills. Take turns listening to each other and "hear" each other. Know when to shut it down and pray if things get out of hand.

Personal Reflection

How can I apply this passage of scripture and nugget to my marriage?

_____

_____

_____

_____

_____

_____

Day 119

If a house is divided against itself, that house cannot stand.
Mark 3:25(NIV)

I like the composer's lyrics to "A House is Not a Home", popularly sung by the late Luther Vandross. Nothing makes sense in that house without the two being together as one. Every component of that house merely exists. The two engaged in the relationship must possess what is needed to unite everything in that house. Without love, compassion, respect, or commitment, that house will NEVER be a home. We can see in the Word of God that homes have been divided since the creation of the family. It takes a lot of work and prayer to keep things in perspective. Without God to assist you when struggles and complications come to your marriage, it will not last. You must have his assistance to keep your hearts and minds in sync. You will need God to keep your marriage fireproof.

Personal Reflection

How am I building my spiritual house and guarding my home?

_____

_____

_____

_____

_____

_____

_____

Day 120

Therefore, my beloved brethren, be ye steadfast, unmovable, always abounding in the work of the Lord, forasmuch as ye know that your labor is not in vain in the Lord.
1 Corinthians 15:58 (KJV)

Sometimes, arguments between two can do irreparable damage to your relationship. It is important for both of you to be careful about how the issue is resolved. If you value what you mean to each other, you will approach your contention in a spirit of love. It comes down to the question of how deep is your love for your spouse. Whatever you're fighting about, is it worth destroying a relationship and degradation of each other? You're in a WAR!! The enemy is out to destroy you and your marriage. Let nothing you're fighting about be the demise of your commitment to each other. You now get to determine your stance. Will you fight for it, or will you allow him to steal and destroy your love for each other? Take the stand to rise against anything that can cause harm to your mate and your marriage. Your rightful place is to stand on the Word of God (speak it!!), pray to him (for his direction), and then walk in obedience to whatever he tells you to do (do it!) Show that a marriage CAN stand in a time such as this!!

Personal Reflection
How am I applying the Word of God in my life and marriage?

_____

_____

_____

_____

_____

_____

Day 121

"In your anger do not sin." *Do not let the sun go down while you are still angry.*
Ephesians 4:26(NIV)

It is a good idea to resolve conflicts as soon as possible. Never go to sleep with unresolved issues. God forbids that one of you won't be awakened to a new day. Some stubborn people choose to let things go on for days, hoping they will go away. In the meantime, so many things are running through your mate's mind, and there are many questions about your love and commitment to each other. The resolution of your conflict is what is essential to both of you, not who's right and who's wrong. Know that you are in this thing together and on the same team. Go into conflict with your armor on. Let prayer be the first step in the resolution of conflict. So, as you grow together, you will find that these conflicts come and go easier every time.

Personal Reflection

How do I use the vehicle of prayer in my marriage? Can I apply this passage of scripture and nugget to my marriage?

_____

_____

_____

_____

_____

_____

Day 122

And why do you look at the speck in your brother's eye,
but do not consider the plank in your own eye?
Matthew 7:3(NKJV)

Being judgmental with your spouse is not a "good look." Who made either of us judge and jury? We bring our own baggage, and my junk isn't any better than yours. In time, we will learn about each other's flaws and shortcomings and learn to adjust or assist our partners in overcoming them. Throwing those things in each other's face can only damage your relationship. Take it to the Lord in prayer. Remember that we are not the "changing agent", God is. He is the only one that can change us, not ourselves. What happened to loving each other unconditionally?

Personal Reflection
How can I apply this passage of scripture and nugget to my marriage?

_____

_____

_____

_____

_____

_____

Day 123

My dear brothers and sisters, take note of this: Everyone should be quick to listen,
slow to speak and slow to become angry.
James 1:19 (NIV)

A lot of times, it's not what you say; it's how you say it. We sometimes answer our spouses in ways that they take as being sarcastic or offensive. It's crucial that before we speak, we should filter the question put to us and use spiritual filters to answer. My wife has told me many times that my response to her, even when I feel she is nagging, makes her feel as if I don't want to be bothered, leading to moments of silence. If there is anyone you do not wish to offend, it's the one you're with. Always be sensitive to how we react or respond to each other. When we don't feel that it's in our best interest to answer at the time, ask your partner for a period to respond. It is courtesy from the other partner that the asked for (time out) is extended to the other. It is so easy sometimes to lash out at each other without thinking what we're going to say, and we end up with stress and tension in the home. ALWAYS THINK BEFORE YOU SPEAK!

Personal Reflection
How am I striving to solve conflict better and speak in love?

_____

_____

_____

_____

_____

Day 124

It is to one's honor to avoid strife, but every fool is quick to quarrel.
Proverbs 20:3(NIV)

Continuous fighting is never good for your relationship or your marriage. Try to head it off at the start. Anything you see that will cause contention or strife in your home. When fighting occurs, do it with a desire to end the conflict quickly. It's not a matter of who wins, but it is resolved in a spirit of love and respect for each other. Always take your partner into consideration by never making accusations or insults. Go into it with a mind of restoring peace to your home. Establish some appropriate rules to back down and go to your neutral corners until both of you are ready to resolve the conflict. When done properly, this will lead to a marriage that will mature and grow and not one of a power struggle.

Personal Reflection
How can I apply this passage of scripture and nugget to my marriage?

_____

_____

_____

_____

_____

_____

Day 125

Live in harmony with one another. Do not be proud,
but be willing to associate with people of low position. Do not be conceited.
Romans 12:16(NIV)

Whenever I think of anything good, I should always have those thoughts for my spouse. They, in my eyes, are everything that's good. Because we are one, we never think or act without the other in mind: one mind, heart, and sound. When we stand together, we are always united as ONE. When we share and give to each other, we help create an atmosphere of intimacy that won't allow us to think selfishly but about the other. Intimacy allows us to come together as ONE.

Personal Reflection
How am I helping to create intimacy and thinking selflessly?

_____

_____

_____

_____

_____

_____

_____

Day 126

Enjoy life with your wife, whom you love, all the days of this meaningless life that God has given you under the sun—all your meaningless days.
For this is your lot in life and in your toilsome labor under the sun.
Ecclesiastes 9:9(NIV)

Life is a gift from God. Therefore, enjoy every passing day with the one you love. James tells us that life is like a vapor; it appears for a while, and then it's gone. Cherish every moment with your partner. Savor their love! Appreciate every morning that you awake to a brand-new dawn as another day to love. If you love hard, there will never be times for regret but memories of wonderful times together. "Precious memories, how they linger."

Personal Reflection
How can I exhibit my love to my spouse as I reflect on each passing day?

_____

_____

_____

_____

_____

_____

Day 127

The heart is deceitful above all things and beyond cure. Who can understand it?
Jeremiah 17:9(NIV)

Sometimes, following our hearts can lead to some messy situations. It could lead to you abandoning your marriage and partner or even delivering the most devastating blow to someone you have vowed to love. God has given each of us the ability to think. We must seek God when making decisions that affect our love for each other and marriage. Our heart is incapable of performing that task. We will seek God. Then and only then can our hearts lead, and it is ONLY then that it will feel right. Take some time during the week or do your date night and watch the movie "Fireproof." It will give you more insight into what it means by the phrase "follow your heart." This movie is for all couples, aspiring couples, and those who have lost the fire in their marriage.

Personal Reflection
How can I apply this passage of scripture and nugget to my marriage?

_____

_____

_____

_____

_____

_____

_____

Day 128

So that with one mind and one voice you may glorify the God
and Father of our Lord Jesus Christ.
Romans 15:6(NIV)

When you look at marriage, see it in a "holistic" way. It would help if you were developed physically, emotionally, mentally, and spiritually. Every aspect of your life requires that both of you are constantly working on the development of each other. It begins with your relationship with your Creator and adhering to His principles regarding being in covenant with the one you have vowed to love for the rest of your days. Work each day to be the husband and wife God expects you to be to each other. Spend quality time together, treat each other with respect, love hard, and learn how to listen to each other. Through this "process, " we grow in the spirit of oneness. This will eventually lead you to a sense of one in mind, heart, body, and spirit. One love, One heartbeat.

Personal Reflection
How can I apply oneness in this passage of scripture to my marriage?

_____

_____

_____

_____

_____

_____

Day 129

Fulfill ye my joy, that ye be like minded, have the same love,
being of one accord, of one mind.
Philippians 2:2(KJV)

True love is relational. You cannot love anyone without a genuine connection. So, we must first remember that love's foundation is built on a healthy friendship. If it's based on sex or infatuation, it will soon crumble. Remember, as we age, things change (shapes, waistlines, and other features). Love is action, it does, it acts! It's more important to demonstrate your love than giving mere lip service. Love is like life; it has its ups and downs. We must share moments when we express what we need from each other. It is healthy to build your love for each other. One of my musical idols in college was the late great Donny Hathaway. When you have an opportunity, please Google and listen to "More Than You Ever Know."

Personal Reflection
How can I apply this passage of scripture and nugget to my marriage?

_____

_____

_____

_____

_____

_____

_____

Day 130

Dear friends, let us love one another, for love come from God.
Everyone who loves has been born of God and knows God.
1 John 4:7(NIV)

The Bible tells the man of the family to love his wife as Christ loved the church. The church is dear to him and is his prize possession upon his return. He gave his life for the church, and this was a love without limits. He loves when this love is reciprocated. This is accomplished through a day-to-day fellowship with him. As we go day to day, the love we have for each other grows stronger. So is our love for our partner; It is nurtured through our constant fellowship and demonstration of our love for each other every day we have together.

We desire that fellowship through wholesome conversation and intimate times together. It makes us long for each other with strong desires to fall in love more each day. Every day you wake is another day God has blessed you to love your spouse. NEVER LET THAT LOVE DIE.

Personal Reflection

How can I love my spouse as Christ loves me and His Church?

_____

_____

_____

_____

_____

_____

Day 131

In this same way, husbands ought to love their wives as their own bodies.
He who loves his wife loves himself.
Ephesians 5:28(NIV)

Do you love your spouse with your whole heart? We should love each other with all our heart, mind, body, and soul, engaging and giving 110% without hesitation or reservation. This kind of love can only come from God, who is love. We must go to him each day and petition him to fill us with love daily. Therefore, always recognize where love comes from. You can't love one another until you first learn to love God. Never let a day go by that you are not reinforcing your love for each other. It is similar to the saying, "where your treasure is, there will your heart be also. Love hard.

Personal Reflection
How can I apply this passage of scripture and nugget to my marriage?

_____

_____

_____

_____

_____

_____

_____

Day 132

Husbands, in the same way be considerate as you live with your wives, and treat them with respect as the weaker partner and as heirs with you of the gracious gift of life, so that nothing will hinder your prayers.
1 Peter 3:7(NIV)

The Word says to give "honor" to whom honor is due. Who else must I give honor to but the one who has had my back for so many years and, with all of my faults and failures, still loves me for who I am. She is truly a virtuous woman because she always puts me before herself. I cherish her because no one can love me like she does. So many times, we take our mates for granted and never consider what they do for us. Today, reflect on how you can honor the one you love. This may be an excellent day to do something special. Do it!!

Personal Reflection
How can I apply this passage of scripture and honor my lover for life?

_____

_____

_____

_____

_____

_____

Day 133

Love must be sincere. Hate what is evil, cling to what is good.
Be devoted to one another in brotherly love. Honor one another above yourselves.
Romans 12:9-10(NIV)

Give honor to your loved one through your respect for them. Let them know that they are special and are of great worth to your life. When you speak to them, let them hear your love. Always be polite. When they request something of you, do your best to fulfill it if possible. It's all about you! Never to hurt you with unkind words or actions that would not honor you as my mate. We are always considerate of each other and find ways to fulfill each other's desires. We accentuate each other because of our love and commitment to each other. Couldn't find this kind of love in another, that's why God gave me YOU!

I have searched all over the world, trying to find that special one
But when I looked into your eyes, I knew you were the one for me
So now I am giving my life to you
So, whatever you want, whatever you need
I am willing and able to give
It's all about you and never about me
("All About You" - Luther Vandross)

Personal Reflection
How can I apply this passage of scripture and nugget to my marriage?

_____

_____

_____

_____

_____

_____

_____

_____

_____

Personal Reflection
Can my spouse hear and feel the love I have for them? How can I apply this nugget to my marriage?

_____

_____

_____

_____

_____

_____

_____

_____

_____

Day 134

Place me like a seal over your heart, like a seal on your arm; for love is as strong as death, its jealousy unyielding as the grave. It burns like blazing fire, like a mighty flame. Many waters cannot quench love; rivers cannot sweep it away. If one were to give all the wealth of one's house for love, it would be utterly scorned.
Song of Solomon 8:6-7(NIV)

Nothing is more important to a couple than their vow to each other on their wedding day. So many have entered this "sacred" union, having no clue what they are getting into. This is a sanctity ordained by God from the beginning of man's existence. The man and the woman become one; we become each other's priority. Jesus said, "For this reason, a man shall leave his father and mother and be joined to his wife, and the two shall become one flesh. So then, they are no longer two but one flesh. Therefore, what God has joined together, let not man separate" (Matthew 19:5,6). The words repeated in our vows are so serious; a vow to "commit" to each other and through your intimacy and relationship, a home is established and a family is born. For us, this is more than a physical union, but also a "spiritual" union. It is the Holy Spirit that will keep our hearts and our minds on "keeping the main thing the main thing", a connection that cannot be separated by anything in this life, but death. We're in it for the long haul.

Personal Reflection
How can I safeguard my marriage and maintain a spiritual union with my spouse?

_____

_____

_____

_____

Day 135

Above all, love each other deeply, because love covers over a multitude of sins.
1 Peter 4:8(NIV)

Love has extended arms; it reaches around and beyond many faults and failures. It survives the best and worst of times and never loses the honor and sacredness of the vows made.

Personal Reflection
How can I apply this passage of scripture and nugget to my marriage?

_____

_____

_____

_____

_____

_____

_____

_____

_____

Day 136

Marriage should be honored by all, and the marriage bed kept pure,
for God will judge the adulterer and all the sexually immoral.
Hebrews 13:4(NIV)

One of the most discouraging events in our society is the dissolution of marriage. It is not being honored by those who take vows to stay in it for the long haul. Marriage has become a social event with no idea of what a covenant relationship really is. We should honor it because it was one of the first institutions sanctioned by God. Our marriage is a commitment to our spouse for a lifetime, keeping yourself ONLY unto them. Nothing and no one can separate us because it was God-ordained. What has happened is that we have allowed our culture to dictate what marriage is rather than sticking to God's original design. Commit to love each other by making God a part of the marriage. God honors us with the gift of marriage and celebrates our union when he is a part of us. Therefore, we should honor marriage with him.

Personal Reflection

How am I honoring my commitment to my marriage and my spouse?

_____

_____

_____

_____

_____

_____

Day 137

*For this cause shall a man leave his father and mother,
and shall be joined unto his wife, and they two shall be one flesh.*
Ephesians 5:31(KJV)

We must learn to love and honor our spouses through our interactions with them and concern for them. Establishing an atmosphere of respect and honor is crucial to developing your marriage and family. When our children can see us demonstrate our love for each other, it will strengthen the whole family. If there is anything that the younger generation needs, it is a "true" example of how marriage is honorable and part of God's original design. The children need to hear your "words of praise" to each other regularly, as this will reinforce their honor and respect for you as parents. It will also illustrate how a husband and wife should treat each other. Appreciating the things that are done, cutting the lawn, cooking, caring for the kids, and maintaining the home will also help you feel valued and important.

Personal Reflection

How is my love demonstrated to my spouse and family each day?

_____

_____

_____

_____

_____

_____

Day 138

Do not be anxious about anything, but in every situation, by prayer and petition,
with thanksgiving, present your requests to God.
Philippians 4:6(NIV)

One of the most important things for a couple is to intercede for each other. Yes, things about us need changing, but that change can only come from the one who created you. Whenever we buy a product that won't work or operate as it should, it is suggested that we return it to the manufacturer. God can change anything; if it cannot be changed, he can change YOU! Make your requests known to him, and watch him go to work on you both. Yes, it's good news to know that when change is needed in our marriages, change can come through our faithful prayers, even when you may feel like you are facing a losing battle. Remember, God can!! It is my prayer that you will find the strength, courage, and faith to do whatever it takes to make your marriage successful. Let God be the changing agent and you the intercessor for your mate. Your prayers are an investment into the transformational process for your loved one. Keep Praying!!!!

Personal Reflection
How can I apply this passage of scripture and nugget to my marriage?

_____

_____

_____

_____

_____

Day 139

Confess your faults one to another, and pray one for another,
that ye may be healed. The effectual fervent prayer of the righteous availeth much.
James 5:16(KJV)

There are many challenges and pressures that face marriages today. Each of us who desires a closer relationship with our spouses must know that it can only be done through the power of prayer. It's all about relationships, but the relationship must start with God. We can't have a horizontal relationship until we first have the vertical relationship with him. Prayer will strengthen our marriages and help us walk together spiritually. The Word says, "How can two walk together unless they agree."

This doesn't mean you and someone else, but you and God. I encourage you to cover your mate in prayer. Pray for their success in their jobs, health, spiritual walk, and walk with God. Make the time to pray together, and those of us with children, pray for and with them. I can truly say that prayer works!! It is one of the most powerful tools a couple could have that is crucial to the survival of marriage and family. The Bible says we ought to always pray.

Personal Reflection

How is prayer a powerful force in my marriage? Why is it important?

_____

_____

_____

_____

_____

Day 140

*Then Jesus told his disciples a parable to show them that they
should always pray and not give up.*
Luke 18:1(NIV)

Marriage requires "staying power", even during struggles and turmoil. At times, we may become discouraged and feel like it's not worth saving, but that, my friend, is a strategy of the enemy to destroy what was ordained from the foundation of the world. How important is it to you to preserve your marriage? It is a battle that can only be won through the power of prayer. It means praying for each other when we are not praying for ourselves. Prayer is not just a one-time thing. For marriage, it is continuous. Your prayers will tear down the walls of selfishness, stubbornness, unforgiveness, and everything that holds your marriage hostage. Stay with it, and never give up.

Personal Reflection
How can I apply this passage of scripture and nugget to my marriage?

_____

_____

_____

_____

_____

_____

_____

Day 141

And we know that all things work together for good to them that love God,
to them who are the called according to his purpose.
Romans 8:28 (KJV)

The sovereignty of God means that he can do anything he wants to do and with whomever he pleases. He is the orchestrator of family and marriage. If there is anyone who can make a difference in the life of your marriage, it is the One who ordained it. Know that if it is broken, He can put the broken pieces back together in your relationship. If we allow him to be Lord of our lives, he can demonstrate and manifest his sovereignty in and through us. Let God be in your marriage. Let him be included in everything you do. He is waiting for us to come to him and allow him to work in our lives. Therefore, it is his will that your marriage should work. Lord, complete the work you have started in my marriage. In Jesus Name.

Personal Reflection

How can I allow God to operate in every area of our marriage?

_____

_____

_____

_____

_____

_____

_____

Day 142

Therefore, confess your sins to each other and pray for each other so that you may be healed. The prayer of a righteous person is powerful and effective.
James 5:16(NIV)

One of the greatest attributes of a relationship is being transparent. You will find no frills, phoniness, or pretenses. You are always honest with each other and love each other just the way you are. You should always be able to be frank and admit your shortcomings and faults, and it is reciprocated to you as well. Your prayers for each other are not just for the moment but are continuous. You never have enough prayers stored on the shelf. There may be times when you can't pray, but because of your consistent prayer life, you can withstand the best and worst of times. Be steadfast in your prayer life and watch how it will sustain your marriage.

Personal Reflection
How can I apply this passage of scripture and nugget to my marriage?

_____

_____

_____

_____

_____

_____

_____

Day 143

If we confess our sins, He is faithful and just to forgive us our sins,
and to cleanse us from all unrighteousness.
1 John 1:9(NKJV)

Your relationship with God is so significant. We need to rid ourselves of all unconfessed sins. Sin creates a barrier between us and God. When this occurs, any petitions to God are hindered. Discord in the home is a definite obstacle to your prayers. When we come to God with a heart of repentance and confession, we can enjoy an open communication channel with him. The Word of God says, "God is faithful and just and will forgive us of our sins and cleanse us of all unrighteousness." Keep your prayer channel clear.

Personal Reflection
How am I finding my way back to God when I feel I have fallen short?

_____

_____

_____

_____

_____

_____

_____

Day 144

Blessed are the peacemakers, for they shall be called the sons of God.
Matthew 5:9(NKJV)

Scolding and nagging is an indication that clear communication has been abandoned. It tells us that our methods of articulating what we want from our partners are off track. Rather than resort to nagging or attempting to discipline your spouse, make your requests known in a more civil manner. It is often not what we say but how we say it that may be offensive to our partner. It is crucial now that they can see it from your perspective, but calmly and not demeaning. Never do anything that will cause a rift in your relationship and marriage. Your job is to keep the lines of communication open with your partner. Remember, you are not the one to change anyone. Only God can do that. Take your concerns to Him and let HIM make the changes. The hymnologist puts it this way: Oh, what peace we often forfeit, oh, what needless pains we bear. All because we do not carry everything to God in prayer.

Personal Reflection

How can I apply this passage of scripture and nugget to my marriage?

_____

_____

_____

_____

_____

_____

Day 145

In the same way, the Spirit helps us in our weakness. We do not know what we ought to pray for, but the Spirit himself intercedes for us through wordless groans. And he who searches our hearts knows the mind of the Spirit, because the Spirit intercedes for God's people in accordance with the will of God.
Romans 8:26-27(NIV)

You should never stop praying for your spouse. Praying is an ongoing process, even when you are angry with each other. When those times come, tell God. When we fail to cover each other in prayer, we open the doors to everything that is divisive and falls apart. The Word of God tells us, "A house divided against itself cannot stand." Prayer will bring about unity in your home and relationship. God has given us the key to success in all we do, and he compels us to "always" pray and not faint. There is no more remarkable example of proving your love for your mate than always lifting them up in prayer. When it seems overwhelming, PUSH!! Pray Until Something Happens!!

Personal Reflection
How can I apply this passage of scripture and develop a better prayer life?

_____

_____

_____

_____

_____

Day 146

Be careful for nothing; but in everything by prayer and supplication
with thanksgivinglet your request be known unto God.
Philippians 4:6(KJV)

There may be situations where you may have a spouse who may not have a personal walk with God. If there is ever a time for prayer, it is now. Your prayers will make a difference for them to have faith in God that can change their lives forever. If you are consistent in your prayer life, you will see them move from faith to faith. Because you love them, you will serve as the covering until they come to the knowledge of who God is. If you continue to pray, you will see God demonstrate His power. The thing you must do is never to give up and know that God will make the difference and not you. Seek his wisdom and watch Him work.

Personal Reflection
How can I apply this passage of scripture and nugget to my marriage?

_____

_____

_____

_____

_____

_____

_____

Day 147

For the weapons of our warfare are not carnal but mighty in God for pulling down strongholds, casting down arguments and every high thing that exalts itself against the knowledge of God, bringing every thought into captivity to the obedience of Christ, and being ready to punish all disobedience when your obedience is fulfilled.
II Corinthians 10:4-6(NKJV)

Many of the issues and struggles we face in our marriages are orchestrated by the enemy to kill, steal, and destroy what was instituted by God. See, the enemy comes in a multiplicity of ways, and it's important that when you pray for your spouse, you cover every area of their life. Satan attempts to affect us in various areas of our lives. Through our health, emotions, walk with God, faith, reputation, and temptations, to name a few. If you are connected with them as you should, you will know what you should pray for. This is more effective when you are praying for each other together. The enemy can't stand it when you are in a spirit of "oneness." But you must know that there is a new "devil", a new devise or scheme to separate you for each new level. Maybe that's why the Word tells us that we ought to "always" pray. Pray without ceasing.

Personal Reflection
How am I using prayer amid struggles and conflict in marriage?

_____

_____

_____

_____

Day 148

But if you do not forgive others their sins, your Father will not forgive your sins.
Matthew 6:15(NIV)

Stay prayed up regarding your spouse. Whatever they need will require them to rely on you and your prayer petition that you put before God. Maintaining an open heart for your marriage will determine your attitude and desire to refrain from lying and being truthful with your spouse. Allow yourself to carry a forgiving spirit instead of bitterness. Bitterness is equivalent to cancer if you allow it to infiltrate your marriage.

Personal Reflection
How can I apply this passage of scripture and nugget to my marriage?

_____

_____

_____

_____

_____

_____

_____

Day 149

Ask and it will be given to you; seek and you will find;
knock and the door will be opened to you.
Matthew 7:7(NIV)

One important thing to remember in a marriage is that we are to always consult God in any and everything we do. This may seem insignificant to you, but with the direction and guidance of God, you cannot go wrong. When God is the foundation of your union together, you should never be reluctant to petition him for things critical to your marriage's success. You have not because you ask not. He is able to supply EVERYTHING you need! Just ASK!!

Personal Reflection
How am I consulting God in my marriage?

_____

_____

_____

_____

_____

_____

_____

Day 150

We know that God does not listen to sinners.
He listens to the godly person who does his will.
John 9:31(NIV)

It is essential to have your ear to the heart of God. Every step you take and every move you make should be in His will. One of the worst things you can do is to operate out of the will of God. Clear direction can only come through a spiritual connection with Him. Proverbs tell us to consult Him in ALL of our ways, and He will give us direction. When we operate without His guidance, we will find that most of our plans and strategies will fail. Connecting to and listening to Him will save you unnecessary heartaches and struggles. Therefore, listen carefully.

Personal Reflection

How can I apply this passage of scripture and nugget to my marriage?

_____

_____

_____

_____

_____

_____

Day 151

Whoever would foster love covers over an offense,
but whoever repeats the matter separates close friends.
Proverbs 17:9(NIV)

In marriage, there are a lot of irritations and imperfections that may rear their heads. This is a natural thing for couples and relationships. The oil of God's anointing is needed daily to cover a multitude of faults and help a marriage survive. Commit to protecting each other for the glory of God and the good of your marriage. You do that by always being mindful of what your mate means to you, and you will not do anything that would destroy the integrity of your marriage or cause each other hurt.

Personal Reflection
How can I apply this passage of scripture and nugget to my marriage?

_____

_____

_____

_____

_____

_____

_____

Day 152

A man who has friends must himself be friendly,
But there is a friend who sticks closer than a brother.
Proverbs 18:24(NKJV)

One of the dearest things in my marriage is my closeness to my mate. There is an unexplainable bond. What makes it so unique is that we were friends first. This means we know each other "intimately," including likes, dislikes, do's and don'ts. When we find time for fellowship, we become one. We gel and do those things that build our love. We share our deepest thoughts and disappointments through our spending quality time together.

Even when I've had a bad day, my mate lends a listening ear to the sequence of events each day. Do you know what makes your mate tick? What drives them? What things attracts them to you intimately? It starts with a friendship, which is the core of any marriage. Start doing something each day to stay connected and to show each other how much you care. A friendship has to be nurtured within your marriage. Friendship is your investment in your mate's emotional, spiritual, and intimate needs within your marriage.

Personal Reflection
How do I consistently seek to hear the heart of my spouse?

_____

_____

_____

_____

_____

Day 153

There is no fear in love. But perfect love drives out fear, because fear has to do with punishment. The one who fears is not made perfect in love.
1 John 4:18(NIV)

A marriage filled with pressure and stress has no place to go but down. Every marriage has its challenges, but when it is filled with stress, many other things are also affected: your intimacy, the atmosphere in your home, and your children. Stress and pressure will cause your relationship and your marriage to deteriorate. This will lead to depression, anxiety, irritability, and the ultimate - DIVORCE. It all goes back to healthy communication between two people. Keeping the best interest of your mate in mind is the key to it all. Our relationships should mean more to us that we will not subject the one we love to unwanted judgment, comparing them to others, or comparing our marriage to another. Those are not good measuring tools! I stand by the notion that RELATIONSHIP is so important. When it breaks down, the enemy will find a way to pick it apart! Know that the two of you are in a growing process of "becoming". Love your mate for who they are, and continue to pray for your marriage. It is an endless job. Keep the faith and stay in the race.

Personal Reflection
How can I work to eliminate stress in my relationship and marriage?

_____

_____

_____

_____

_____

Day 154

Make every effort to keep the unity of the Spirit through the bond of peace.
Ephesians 4:3(NIV)

The Bee Gees wrote a song entitled "How Deep Is Your Love" that expresses the depth of love felt for one's love. It describes a feeling that goes beyond our surface thinking. A love that makes you feel safe, even when life's elements try to break you down; you still know to whom you belong. Often, the depth of love is hindered because of the mistakes made and things that may have hurt us; these things can add stress to you. I can't find the tools to measure my love. We're a team, even though we have different personalities and identities, we can love each other just as we are. Imperfect we may be, but we should love each other, knowing that in nurturing our relationship, we will create a bond that nothing and no one will be able to separate. Love comes with its share of baggage, but the question is whether or not you're in it for the long haul. Stay committed to the notion that you are bound to fulfill your covenant with them "until death do us part."

Personal Reflection
How can I apply this passage of scripture and nugget to my marriage?

_____

_____

_____

_____

_____

_____

Day 155

I am my beloved's and my beloved is mine.
Song of Solomon 6:3(KJV)

This verse is from one of the wisest men in the world who speaks to the very essence of God's original plan for a man and a woman; "and two became one flesh" (Genesis 2:24). Two hearts beating as one, a union which the tie of marriage brings on. No more are we separate, but when we are in communion and relationship with each other through marriage, we are covenant partners. This is a mutual union between you and your spouse and a commitment to each other. I feel what you feel, I hurt when you hurt, I rejoice in your success, and vice versa. This is accomplished through unified hearts and minds, first united with the author and creator of marriage.

Personal Reflection

How can I apply this passage of scripture and nugget to my marriage?

_____

_____

_____

_____

_____

_____

Day 156

Blessed are those who find wisdom, those who gain understanding.
Proverbs 3:13(NIV)

Wisdom reminds you of what is most important to us: love, patience, tolerance, forgiveness, and commitment. Wisdom helps us not to overreact, pass judgment, or point fingers. It will help us put things in perspective. True wisdom comes only from God. The Bible declares that the Lord gives wisdom, and out of his mouth comes knowledge and understanding. Our natural wisdom will lead us to make bad choices and decisions. If we seek God's wisdom, we find ourselves in a better position to handle those things that can be detrimental to our relationship and marriage. You can't find it anywhere else but in God. Ask for it.

Personal Reflection
How can I apply this passage of scripture and nugget to my marriage?

_____

_____

_____

_____

_____

_____

Day 157

Place me like a seal over your heart, like a seal on your arm;
for love is as strong as death, its jealousy unyielding as the grave.
It burns like a blazing fire, like a mighty flame.
Song of Solomon 8:6(NIV)

One of the most essential things in marriage is knowing everything about your mate. How do you know if you are not sleeping with the enemy? When I know my mate, I know all of the intricate details about them. During moments of intimacy (in-to-me-see) we learn what makes our mates tick. What are their wants, desires, and needs? This leads me to my next point for those who are anticipating marriage. Learn to be friends first!! One of the most significant advantages of my relationship with my wife is that we were friends first. It helped in building the strong bond that exists between us today. There is NOTHING that I go through or experience that I can't share with her. It is key to your relationship and marriage. Learn all you can about your mate. It will reveal so much of what you need to learn and know about them.

Personal Reflection
How can I apply this passage of scripture and nugget to my marriage?

_____

_____

_____

_____

_____

Day 158

Who can find a virtuous woman? For her price is above rubies.
Proverbs 31:10(KJV)

What made your heart flutter when you first saw your mate? Was it their smile, looks, personality, or physique? Did you have the opportunity to "study" your mate and find out what makes them tick? It always goes back to relationship building. This can only happen when you become "friends." The horrible error of many marriages today is selecting someone for the wrong reasons, and the relationship ends in you needing to know all of the intricate details about the one you want to spend your life with. Don't rush it!! Like a marriage, it takes time.

To the woman dating, it's not good for you to go looking. Your request should be made known to God as to choosing your mate. You (ladies) often go out hunting, and what you bring back is not good for you. After you've made your request known to God, let him find you. You wait patiently on the Lord, and He will deliver.

To the man dating, your request should be the same. Let God lead you to your wife, and don't always go on what you "see." What you see most of the time is deceiving. You've got to study her. To those of us who are still in it to win it; whatever got the fire started, keep it burning and yearning. Your love for each other is an eternal flame.

Personal Reflection

How am I using prayer amid struggles and conflict in marriage?

_____

_____

_____

_____

_____

_____

_____

_____

_____

_____

Personal Reflection
How am I seeking God's guidance in my marriage?

_____

_____

_____

_____

_____

_____

_____

Day 159

Dear children, let us not love with words or speech, but with actions and in truth.
1 John 3:18(NIV)

Intimacy is the first step toward studying your mate. It's more than sex, it's about getting into the psyche of your mate: their thoughts, concerns, anxieties, and desires. Your relationship is strengthened when you spend time with each other. This may mean doing the unexpected: a getaway or a romantic evening with your lover - without the children. The sky is the limit for those of us with an empty nest. By studying your mate, you'll know what arouses them, turns them on, and turn them off. You can tell them you love them, but you can deepen your intimacy and connection with your spouse by exploring. Use your imagination and do it!!

Personal Reflection

How am I finding time to spend with my spouse to create intimacy?

_____

_____

_____

_____

_____

_____

_____

Day 160

Entreat me not to leave you, or to turn back from following after you; for wherever you go, I will go; and wherever you lodge, I will lodge; Your people shall be my people, and your God, my God. Where you die, I will die, and there will I be buried. The Lord do so to me, and more also, if anything but death parts you and me.
Ruth 1:16-17(NKJV)

When you first were married, you inherited a mate or partner with different values, likes, dislikes, and a different belief system. Studying anything entails knowing the details. What makes them tick? What upsets them, causes undo stress, and makes them appreciate your marriage?

This is important because we should always travel the same paths, avoiding those things that can tear our relationship and marriage apart. We want to be deeply connected and compatible with each other. Our connection consists of a lifelong commitment, a lifelong desire to love everything about each other, and knowing every intricate detail about our lover for life. You will experience an ongoing process each day of your lives together. Studying each other is ongoing - till death do us part.

Personal Reflection
How can I apply this passage of scripture and nugget to my marriage?

_____

_____

_____

_____

_____

Day 161

And the two become one flesh. So, they are no longer two, but one flesh.
Therefore, what God has joined together, let no one separate.
Mark 10:8-9(NIV)

Do you have a favorite movie or a movie that you can watch over and over again? It does something for you every time you watch. There is always some small or intimate detail that you discover in every viewing. We should do the same with our marriages and relationships. It's always up for review. It might be the small detail that makes our intimacy more intimate. We may have forgotten some scenes from our own movie, and our partner is wondering where it all went. Our job is to be in continuous study of our partners for life, always seeking ways to keep the marriage vibrant and alive. If my mate means that much to me, I will do whatever it takes to find my way back to those things that make them happy.

Personal Reflection
How am I learning more about my spouse to better our marriage and relationship?

_____

_____

_____

_____

_____

_____

Day 162

The heart of the discerning acquires knowledge, for the ears of the wise seek it.
Proverbs 18:15(NIV)

One of the hardest things for men is being able to listen to their wives. If we would only take that time and listen closely, they would tell us all of the things that are important to them that we tend to pay little attention to. What annoys them, what moves them, what interests them? All of these questions can be answered if we would listen. However, listening is a two-way street. If you differ in opinions and views in your listening, don't take it personally because we think differently and come from different backgrounds. In our listening, both of us should pay attention to details. Hear every part of the conversation.

Response: I hear you when you say .... Are you saying ....?

These statements will show that what they say is important and that you are concerned about what actions, comments, or gestures have affected them. Give them that assurance every time it's needed, even when it is not what you want to say. Remember, what you give out will return to you.

Personal Reflection
How can I apply this passage of scripture and nugget to my marriage?

_____

_____

_____

_____

_____

Day 163

The wise store up knowledge, but the mouth of a fool invites ruin.
Proverbs 10:14(NIV)

Another critical point for all of us who are married is that we do not say anything that would be damaging to our mate. Furthermore, we need to think before we act and listen before we speak. That is demonstrating wisdom. The tongue, at times, is uncontrollable and is the cause of many who walk away from relationships because what is said causes so much damage. Remember, wisdom comes from God. Whenever you seek ways to deal with any situation in your marriage, seek God's wisdom. Wisdom will cause you to do things differently and internalize things differently. It won't let your words cause harm to the one you love, but it will cause you to be attentive and concerned about what's important to you – your soul mate.

Personal Reflection
How can I consult God in times of conflict?

_____

_____

_____

_____

_____

_____

Day 164

For the Lord gives wisdom, from his mouth come knowledge and understanding.
Proverbs 2:6 (NIV)

Two lives become one, and two personalities mesh. Two backgrounds merge into one. We respect what each other brings to the table and value them as well. Nothing about my mate is meaningless. Every thought, opinion, and suggestion are important to me. It's because we are two individuals desiring to have one heart and sound. We can never be sure that we will make the right decisions in our marriage. It can only come with having spiritual discernment. The Word says that if we acknowledge Him in all that we do, He will give us the wisdom to make sound decisions. Seek God in knowing your partner's mind, heart, and innermost desires. He'll make it plain.

Personal Reflection
How can I apply this passage of scripture and nugget to my marriage?

_____

_____

_____

_____

_____

_____

Day 165

By wisdom a house is built, and through understanding it is established; through knowledge its rooms are filled with rare and beautiful treasures.
Proverbs 24:3-4(NIV)

An important process in building a house's structure is its foundation. If the foundation is shaky, the structure will eventually shift and cause damage to the home. When our marriage is not built on wisdom, love, and trust, our relationship has an unstable foundation. We know that wisdom doesn't come from our intuitions but from the only source that can give it: God Himself. If we center our marriages and homes on the wisdom of God, He will guide us into all truths. Every attack of the enemy on the structure of our marriage will be ineffective. If His wisdom leads us, each room of our house (our marriage) will consist of whatever is necessary for its survival. The bottom line is that our marriages and homes must be established on the Word of God, and knowledge is knowing what to do with it. Stay on guard and hide the Word in your heart.

Personal Reflection
How am I establishing a godly foundation in protecting my marriage?

_____

_____

_____

_____

_____

_____

Day 166

Many women do noble things, but you surpass them all.
Proverbs 31:29(NIV)

There is a familiar phrase in the opening of one of my favorite childhood shows, Star Trek. It says, "to boldly go where no man has ever gone before." For us men to win at marriage, we must find the hearts of our wives to focus on their needs and those things that move or motivate them. It's like any sport. You may have the determination, heart, and motivation, but you'll never win if you don't have the skills. You've got to dig DEEPER! When you've found her heart, you've found a gold mine. Proverbs says it so plainly: An excellent wife who can find? The heart of her husband trusts in her, and he will have no lack of gain. She does him good and does not harm all the days of her life. Strength and dignity are her clothing, and she laughs at the days to come. Her children rise up and call her blessed; her husband also praises her. Men, have you found your wife's heart?

Dig deeper!!

Personal Reflection
How am I consistently establishing the trust of my spouse?

_____

_____

_____

_____

_____

_____

Day 167

The beginning of wisdom is this: Get wisdom.
Though it cost all you have, get understanding.
Proverbs 4:7(NIV)

A true connection with your spouse is necessary because your love for them is the core of your relationship. You can see through the masks and facades you sometimes experience, yet you see in the midst of all that the true essence of the one you love. When we love each other, it is not about that person filling the void in your life, but that with your mate, you feel complete.

As for men, the women in our lives complement us. That is why the Word says being alone is not good for us (men). You both realize that you have differences and similarities. Still, a gap exists, and it causes us to consistently explore those unchartered areas needed to build the love, honor, and respect that will outlast anything you face.

Intimacy is necessary for you to develop a relationship. Remember that it's more than sex. It is the mixing of two hearts. God has designed it so that we long for intimacy with Him. Therefore, it is by His divine providence that we connect. Dig!!

Personal Reflection

How am I working to ensure my connection to my spouse?

_____

_____

_____

_____

_____

Day 168

And so, we know and rely on the love God has for us. God is love.
Whoever lives in love, lives in God, and God in them.
1 John 4:16 (NIV)

One writer defines unconditional love as a love that has no limits, an element of love and affection that supersedes any faults or flaws. This type of love is not grounded on looks or expectations but on the premise that nothing and no one can separate you from each other. It is based on how we treat each other, with ground rules to handle days of conflict, days of want, and days of plenty. To help us understand this kind of love, we must first look at how God sees us; with our many faults and shortcomings, He looks beyond all these things and loves us anyway. Ephesians 5:1-2 tells us that we are to be imitators of God's love and demonstrate that same kind of love in our relationship. His love story is the best "love" story ever told. Dig Deeper!!

Personal Reflection
How can I apply this passage of scripture and nugget to my marriage?

_____

_____

_____

_____

_____

_____

Day 169

For all have sinned and fall short of the glory of God.
Romans 3:23(NIV)

Today, it is vital for all of us to self-evaluate ourselves. Where do you stand with your relationship with God and with one another? If we don't have a horizontal relationship with each other, it's impossible for us to have a vertical relationship with God. If we say we love God, it is easy to love our fellow man, no matter what. When we violate this command, it hinders our relationship with God and each other. It also hinders our prayer life, and our requests to God will meet unwanted delays. This is a good day for a check-up. Take a look at your love life with your spouse as well as your fellow man. See if you are in line with the great command Christ has given all of us to live by. Having no love is like distortion on the telephone line; there is never a true connection. Love hard!!

Personal Reflection
What is my relationship with my Creator? How do I maintain my relationship with Him?

_____

_____

_____

_____

_____

_____

Day 170

Dear friends, let us love one another, for love comes from God.
Everyone who loves has been born of God and knows God.
1 John 4:7(NIV)

What's love got to do with it? What is it that I need that will help me to keep on loving someone during hurt, betrayal, disappointment, and insurmountable marital pressure? The nature of man alone cannot find it within himself to love like this. This love can only come from God. We can never find it within ourselves to love this way. It can only come with the aid and help of God and His spirit that lives within us. Try Christ when you feel like you need that little boost to go beyond your human frailties. He can give you a love that goes beyond your understanding. It's all because it is the essence of who He is – LOVE. As the writer in John infers, you can't do it by yourself; without Him, we can do NOTHING.

Personal Reflection
How can I apply this passage of scripture and nugget to my marriage?

_____

_____

_____

_____

_____

_____

Day 171

If you remain in me and my words remain in you,
ask whatever you wish, and it will be done for you.
John 15:7(NIV)

There are a lot of things that you may desire in your relationship and marriage. They may include the safety and protection of your family, a strong connection between you and your spouse, or the wisdom of God in your decision-making. This can only be accomplished by staying connected to God and abiding by His will for your relationship and marriage. When our marriages follow the blueprint established by God, we can be assured that our needs and some of our desires are granted. We must make it our business to stay connected to the One who can supply us with ALL we need for a fulfilling relationship and marriage. All things are possible with Him, and without being connected to Him, we will surely fail. Stay connected!!

Personal Reflection

How am I praying for the survival and needs of my marriage?

_____

_____

_____

_____

_____

_____

Day 172

Now to him who is able to do immeasurably more than all we ask or imagine,
according to his power that is at work within us.
Ephesians 3:20(NIV)

Sometimes, during our marriage, we reach rough spots and obstacles that we think will cause the demise of our relationship. But because of our connection with Him, we can conquer and withstand whatever. That means that He has endowed us with the power of the Holy Spirit. The Holy Spirit will equip us to handle whatever comes our way. It's powerful and explosive and will help you reach beyond the natural to the supernatural, knowing that He (our Creator) can do far more than our finite minds can apprehend or comprehend. It's all in the connection.

Personal Reflection
How can I apply this passage of scripture and nugget to my marriage?

_____

_____

_____

_____

_____

_____

Day 173

For I know the thoughts that I think toward you, saith the Lord,
thoughts of peace, and not of evil, to give you an expected end.
Jeremiah 29:11(KJV)

Acts 17:28(NIV) makes it so plain to us in reference to our very existence on planet Earth. It says, "For in Him," we live and move and have our being. This means to me that every breath that I breathe is dependent upon God. Why wouldn't I depend solely on Him regarding my marriage and relationship if He is my source? He has orchestrated every obstacle, success, peak, and valley in our marriage. If I trust Him completely, all I have to do is to go along for the ride and let Him lead the way. It is God who has established and ordained the sanctity of marriage. If we release our mates, our children, and all of our affairs to Him, He'll make EVERYTHING alright. The hymn writer writes, "Tis so sweet to trust in Jesus. Just to take Him at His word. Just to rest upon His promise; Just to know thus said the Lord." Trust Him today.

Personal Reflection
How am I trusting God in every area of my life?

_____

_____

_____

_____

_____

_____

Day 174

With man this is impossible, but with God all things are possible.
Matthew 19:26(NIV)

At some time, we would say that we've experienced true love or found our true love. It's hard to find a definition for true love in the natural. It can only be found in God Himself. Our love is sometimes conditional and subject to our personal emotions. For us to deal with the misfortunes of marriage and relationships, we can only get through these times by having a connection with the only true example of love. Being connected with God can help us withstand many bumps and bruises that we experience in a relationship. It helps us forgive when it can be so difficult in the natural world. Recognize where you can get what you need to help you give true love and experience it in your marriage. This is the kind of love that can hold things together.

Personal Reflection
How is the love of God being demonstrated in my life and marriage?

_____

_____

_____

_____

_____

_____

Day 175

For the Son of man came to seek and to save the lost.
Luke 19:10(NIV)

There is a song by a quartet group that says, "If Jesus can't fix it, nobody can." We have two imperfect individuals trying to fix something they can't. Whenever you purchase items that stores can't repair, it is suggested that it is returned to the manufacturer. When our marital affairs are out of whack, we should give our concerns and petitions to the one who made us. Only He can make it right. Sometimes, things can be a little more than we can handle in our marriages. Turn them over to Jesus, and He can work it out. He can do exceedingly and abundantly above all that we can ask or think, according to the POWER that worketh in us. Believe me, He is able.

Personal Reflection

What do I do when we are experiencing turmoil? Where do I turn?

_____

_____

_____

_____

_____

_____

Day 176

*He Himself bore our sins" in His body on the cross,
so that we might die to sins and live for righteousness;
by His wounds you have been healed*
1 Peter 2:24(NIV)

How much are you willing to sacrifice for the happiness of your partner? How important is their happiness to you? Love is giving until it hurts. It is not selfish but seeks to satisfy one's desires. Ephesians tells us we should love our wives as Christ loves the church. This kind of love is the most genuine model of what Christ expects from those of us who are lifetime lovers. This means that I will take the initiative to love my spouse with the desire to provide for them emotionally, relationally, physically, and spiritually. You are my heart's desire.

Personal Reflection

How far will I go to show my love to my spouse?

_____

_____

_____

_____

_____

_____

Day 177

Let us not become weary in doing good,
for at the proper time we will reap a harvest if we do not give up.
Galatians 6:9(NIV)

I choose to love my spouse with all of their faults and frailties. Whatever it takes to prove my love for her is my driving force. It includes making them my priority and committing to their happiness. As my vows state, I promise to love, honor, and cherish her for the rest of my earthly existence. It is our job to fulfill our responsibilities to our partners with the help of God. Vow to commit to a lifelong marriage regardless of what comes your way. Paul reflected on his relationship with Christ by saying, "I will let nothing separate me from the love." Choose to love. Our journey together is not only possible, but it starts and ends with love and commitment.

Personal Reflection

How far will I go to ensure the safety and security of our relationship?

_____

_____

_____

_____

_____

_____

Day 178

Trust in the Lord with all your heart, and lean not on your own understanding.
In all your ways acknowledge Him, and He shall direct your path.
Proverbs 3:5-6(NKJV)

One of the greatest gifts we have experienced is the love God gives us. Despite all of our shortcomings, He still loves and cares for us. Even when we have turned our backs on Him in search of our desires, He is still the epitome of love by reclaiming us back to Him. True love looks beyond what we see and think and loves anyway. It says I love you, and I long to be around you. Even when we've had our differences, there's no one I would rather be with than you. It's caring for your mate spiritually, physically, and emotionally. Treasure the special bond you share with your mate and do whatever you can to make them happy. We don't deserve the love God gives us, yet He still loves us. Stay in love regardless of the bumps and bruises of marriage. It's a full-time job and a continual process, but it's worth working through whatever with the one YOU love.

Personal Reflection
How am I working to keep my marriage vibrant and thriving?

_____

_____

_____

_____

_____

_____

Day 179

The Lord will guide you always; He will satisfy your needs in a sun-scorched land and will strengthen your frame. You will be like a well-watered garden, like a spring whose waters never fail.
Isaiah 58:11 (NIV)

The course of a marriage is like treading unchartered waters; there will be some highs and lows. We need to realize that we can't make this journey by ourselves. The Word tells us that if we consult God in all that we do, He will give us the directives we need to survive the many unnecessary setbacks we might face. When we let Him take the lead, He can take every trial and struggle we face to draw to Him and each other. If we only delight ourselves in Him, He will give us the desires of our hearts. If our desire is to fulfill our commitment to each other, we can best withstand the highs and lows and beat all odds. Nothing is impossible with God if we only place Him in the formula. If you are committed to each other, remain committed to seek God as you journey through matrimony. Let's do this!!

Personal Reflection

How am I consulting God in every aspect of our relationship?

_____

_____

_____

_____

_____

_____

Day 180

Being confident of this very thing, that He which has begun
a good work in you will complete it until the day of Jesus Christ.
Philippians 1:6(NKJV)

In our marital selection process, we sometimes place high expectations on the chosen man or woman. Sometimes it's done with the thinking that the person we choose is what we think we want or can be groomed to what we want and desire. By just self-evaluating, we will soon realize we are imperfect people on the potter's wheel. Each day, God molds and shapes us into what He has designed us to be. It is not our right to place our personal demands on our mates based on our understanding. Each of us in marriage comes with our own imperfections. Let God do His perfect work in us individually and collectively as a couple. It is only He who is able to change the hearts and the ways of man. If things need to be changed in your marriage, turn it over to Jesus, He'll fix it. I promise when He has completed the work, you can honestly say God did it.

Personal Reflection
How can I apply this passage of scripture and nugget to my marriage?

_____

_____

_____

_____

_____

Day 181

Do not be anxious about anything, but in every situation, by prayer and petition, with thanksgiving, present your requests to God. And the peace of God, which transcends all understanding, will guard your hearts and your minds in Christ Jesus.
Philippians 4:6-7(NIV)

There was a song we sang when I was young that said, "without God, I could do nothing, without Him I'd surely fail." It told me that everything I do depends on my trust in God and what He can do. When we were young, we relied on our parents to supply us with our needs; most of the time, they came through. But our God is Jehovah Jireh. All we need to sustain us in marriage rests upon our faith in a God who can provide for our every need. Rest in knowing that He is in control, which means that we can comfortably give Him all our anxieties, requests, plans, and desires to handle. Rest on the promises of God and what He has designed marriage to be. Give it to Jesus, and He will give you peace that passes all understanding.

Personal Reflection
How am I demonstrating my dependency on God? Is it working in me?

_____

_____

_____

_____

_____

_____

Day 182

I know what it is to be in need, and I know what it is to have plenty. I have learned the secret of being content in any and every situation, whether well fed or hungry, whether living in plenty or in want. I can do all this through him who gives me strength.
Philippians 4:12-13(NIV)

In my short time on planet Earth, I have learned that our Creator carefully orchestrates everything we go through. It is all part of our process and is designed to mold and shape us into what God has prepared for our lives. Every struggle and trial bring lessons to help us grow spiritually and emotionally. There will be instances where we will face dark days unannounced, out of nowhere; that's when we can gain strength in sharing the pain and looking to God for help to get through it. In Him, we have the calm assurance that we are not in this thing alone. Stand firm together as one, knowing that when the dust settles, you can look to God and say, we never would've made it without Him.

Personal Reflection

How do I know that God is a part of my marriage? Do I make room for Him?

_____

_____

_____

_____

_____

_____

Day 183

And my God will meet all your needs according to the riches of his glory in Christ Jesus.
Philippians 4:19(NIV)

Just as God is the supplier of all our needs, our marital needs should only be supplied by our mate. Neither of us should search for anything or anyone outside to fill our voids. That is why communication is so vital to your relationship. Your spouse will only know your wants and needs if they are verbally addressed. They can't be assumed or guessed but expressed. Let your requests be known!!

Personal Reflection
How can I apply this passage of scripture and nugget to my marriage?

_____

_____

_____

_____

_____

_____

_____

Day 184

When thou passest through the waters, I will be with thee; and through the rivers, they shall not overflow thee: when thou walkest through the fire, thou shall not be burned; neither shall the flame kindle upon thee.
Isaiah 43:2(KJV)

Fortunately, we have a God who remains the same; He never changes. In our marriage, things will change, and things will occur that may affect us suddenly. We are blessed to serve a God that can handle our worst situations. What is important is that we stay connected to Him. He has proven that He is faithful to us in whatever, whenever.

Personal Reflection
How does God show His faithfulness to me and my marriage?

_____

_____

_____

_____

_____

_____

_____

Day 185

Take delight in the Lord, and he will give you the desires of your heart.
Psalm 37:4(NIV)

One of the advantages of a good marriage is having two individuals with a relationship with God, not just a casual relationship, but a true knowledge of who God is. When your priorities lie in honoring God and walking in His purpose, you will witness God in His fullness. If He is first, you have a guarantee that He will not only provide you with all of your needs but it will include some of your heart's desire. These will always line up in the will of God. He's got to be number one; anything else is idolatry. Take the time to discuss with your mate what's important in your marriage. If God is in the plan, you can be assured that He will satisfy your every need.

Personal Reflection
Where does God fit in my marriage and my life?

_____

_____

_____

_____

_____

_____

_____

Day 186

The steps of a good man are ordered by the Lord: and he delighteth in his way.
Psalm 37:23(KJV)

If God orders our steps, we should look to Him, knowing He orchestrates our whole life. The Word tells us in 1 Peter 5:7 that we should never be anxious but make our requests known to the only one who can supply all our needs. We should never worry if we have truly turned everything over to God. He had our best interest in mind when He created the institution of marriage. Use those things we experience in marriage as stepping stones to prepare us for His purpose. Trust Him to give you everything you need in your marriage. Hold on to God's unchanging hand, knowing that our times are in His hand.

Personal Reflection
How do I consult God and use our experiences to help us grow?

_____

_____

_____

_____

_____

_____

_____

Day 187

You open your hand and satisfy the desires of every living thing.
Psalm 145:16(NIV)

David's desire in this Psalm is to express the goodness and provisions of God in a portrait of praise. He recognizes the sovereignty of God and what He has been to him and all people. God is acknowledged as the One who can supply the needs of all of us. When we look at our marriage and relationship with God, we can truly trust that God will fulfill every promise He has made us. If we are faithful to the cause of marriage, He will open His hand and satisfy our every need and desire. Today, praise God for what He has done in your marriage thus far. Even though it hasn't always been rosy, He has kept us through good and bad times. He has been true to the commitment that He would never leave us nor forsake us. Every day should be a day of praise for what He has done in our marriages. We never could have made it without Him. Give Him praise!!

Personal Reflection

How am I demonstrating my faithfulness to God and my spouse?

_____

_____

_____

_____

_____

_____

Day 188

For God so loved the world that he gave his one and only Son,
that whoever believes in him shall not perish but have eternal life.
John 3:16(NIV)

Love is one of the building blocks of a marriage. It overshadows all the faults and failures that may occur together during the lifetime. We love each other because of and never in spite of. When we married, we knew we both brought many imperfections with us. However, because of the example given to us by our Lord and Savior, we can look beyond all of our shortcomings and still find love. God commands love. When it is present in our marriages, they are complete. Like mercy, it is new every morning. When we awake and see the gift of another day, it's good to know that God has allowed us the opportunity to see love next to us. Cherish your love for each other and take time each day to renew it. When everything else fails, love NEVER fails.

Personal Reflection
How can I apply this passage of scripture and nugget to my marriage?

_____

_____

_____

_____

_____

Day 189

Let love and faithfulness never leave you; bind them around your neck,
write them on the tablet of your heart. Then you will win favor and a good name
in the sight of God and man.
Proverbs 3:3-4(NIV)

There is a nugget in the Book of Wisdom that says, "let love and faithfulness never leave you; bind them around your neck and write them upon the tables of your heart." When you are faithful to something or someone, you are sold out with everything within you. Everything about that person is important to you. Your love for them goes beyond every boundary and exceeds our deepest thoughts and feelings.

Our faithfulness to each other is not just a one-time thing, but it is reiterated and practiced each day we are together. We hold our love for each other dear to us, and nothing can shake the foundation of what we have. When we make our promises, we vow to always consider our mate's well-being. Faithfulness is a serious marital issue. Tom Houck says it this way, "To commit to someone for five minutes is easy, but to commit to someone for a lifetime is a much stronger commitment."

Personal Reflection

How committed am I to remain faithful to my marriage for as long as we live?

_____

_____

_____

_____

_____

Day 190

By this everyone will know that you are my disciples, if you love one another.
John 13:35(NIV)

Love is as love does. It is not merely said but is demonstrated in how we express our love for each other. When love is real, it is not pretentious or phony but is portrayed in your smile, your glances, and the ambiance of being in each other's presence. It can't be manufactured or faked. Love is like a seed; it is planted and grows and blossoms. What results is a series of sitting with each other, laughing with each other, enjoying each other, hugging, and kissing each other. Love has a look, and you will know it when you see it.

Personal Reflection
How can I apply this passage of scripture and nugget to my marriage?

_____

_____

_____

_____

_____

_____

_____

Day 191

Owe no one anything, except to love one another,
for he who loves another has fulfilled the law.
Romans 13:8(NKJV)

Thank God for the gift of love. Whether it is received or not, it is still available to us. In our attempts to love each other without limits, there will be times when we must display the agape love that Christ speaks of. Is it easy when you have been hurt, betrayed, or taken for granted? Check yourself today and ask yourself about the measure of love that is exhibited in your marriage. As Christ has remained faithful to us, so should we be with our spouses. It's all a part of our process.

Personal Reflection
How can I apply this passage of scripture and nugget to my marriage?

_____

_____

_____

_____

_____

_____

Day 192

But to you who are listening I say: Love your enemies, do good to those who hate you,
bless those who curse you, pray for those who mistreat you.
Luke 6:27-28(NIV)

When we look at the enemy, there are a few things that we should always be mindful of. It is that our marriage will always be under attack by the enemy. Pray that God will give you the discernment to identify when the enemy is attacking your marriage. Many times, if we allow him to, the enemy will use us to do his bidding. If you are prayerful about your marriage, it is easily recognized. The Word of God says, "We wrestle not against flesh and blood, but against principalities, against powers, against the rulers of darkness of this world, against spiritual wickedness in high places." Know what you're fighting against. He will use us if we are available. If we are abounding in the love of Christ, it is easy to love those who come against us, personally and in our marriage. We can stand flat-footed and proclaim, I love you in spite of. Walk in His love!!

Personal Reflection

How am I safeguarding my marriage against the attacks of the enemy?

_____

_____

_____

_____

_____

_____

Day 193

*In Him we have redemption through his blood, the forgiveness of sins,
in accordance with the riches of God's grace.*
Ephesians 1:7(NIV)

Love covers a multitude of faults and failures. It transcends every hardship and makes the best of every situation. Jesus demonstrates His compassion for us, wherein He looks beyond our blemishes with a love that remains faithful to us. Love is the essence of who God is. Who better could be the greatest example of how we should love and be devoted to the ones we love. It is a commitment for life, to love, and to cherish. It has no conditions but is patient and longsuffering. It will last.

Personal Reflection
How do I show grace to the one I love? Is it consistent?

_____

_____

_____

_____

_____

_____

_____

Day 194

If you love those who love you, what credit is that to you? Even sinners love those who love them. And if you do good to those who are good to you,
what credit is that to you? Even sinners do that.
Luke 6:32-33(NIV)

Your love for your spouse should not be contingent upon what you are given, that's conditional. Love should be unconditional. I love you because of. Not for the things being done for you but because of who you are. It's like our love for God. We should love Him not for what He can give us but for WHO He is. That type of love is special. Love is what we expect from each other. When it stops or changes, it affects both of us. If we have to do something special or act a certain way for it to be given to us, it's not real love. We need to remember that when love is given and given freely, we will find that it is reciprocated to us. Give it, and it shall be given to you.

Personal Reflection
How do I demonstrate unconditional love to my spouse?

_____

_____

_____

_____

_____

_____

Day 195

But love your enemies, do good to them, and lend to them without expecting to get anything back. Then your reward will be great, and you will be children of the Most High, because he is kind to the ungrateful and wicked.
Luke 6:35(NIV)

My actions reflect how I feel for my spouse. Because my love for them is so strong, I never expect anything in return but their love. Giving it from the heart opens up every possibility because it conquers hate. Love is forgiving; when necessary, it covers hurt, even when we fall short. A writer once wrote, "Love is most valuable to the giver when given freely and without thought." It shall be returned to you.

Personal Reflection
How can I apply this passage of scripture and nugget to my marriage?

_____

_____

_____

_____

_____

_____

Day 196

Beloved, let us love one another, for love is of God,
and everyone that loveth is born of God, and knoweth God.
1 John 4:7(KJV)

We should be the essence of who God is. He is love. Whether we wanted to be loved or not, He loved us so much to make concessions for all of us through Jesus Christ, the greatest example of His love. Sometimes, we fall short in our marriages where we need love to prevail.

Though we are not deserving, our love for each other will keep us even when the bottom seems to fall out. This can never be accomplished in us if we are not connected to God. Only through Him can we love when we find it so hard to do. Many times, our love is based on feelings and emotions, but if we have the sure love of God, when we feel like we've fallen out of love, with Him, we can love again.

Personal Reflection

How can I love my spouse as God shows His love to me?

_____

_____

_____

_____

_____

_____

Day 197

My little children, let us not love in word neither in tongue, but in deed and in truth.
1John 3:18(KJV)

It is amazing to witness the undeserved love of God each day. The hymn writer says "Great is thy faithfulness." Each new morning brings with it God's love for an undeserving people, yet it is permeated to the world despite who we are and what we've done. God has given us love so that we too can give it to whoever needs it. Give it freely, not only to your spouse but let it be a part of who you are in God; an expression of love, for while we were yet sinners, He loved us so much that He gave His life. Your mate should witness your love each morning. A love so strong that it says to them, that I love you with all the imperfections that you have. Knowing this, you can be the most remarkable example of WHO and WHAT God is. He is the epitome of Love.

Personal Reflection
How has God been faithful to me and my marriage?

_____

_____

_____

_____

_____

_____

Day 198

And now these three remain: faith, hope and love. But the greatest of these is love.
I Corinthians 13:13(NIV)

Love is much more than sparks or feelings. They are both temporal and will not last. When they are the foundation of our marriages, love will eventually fade, and we become cohabitants rather than partners. When love is paired with fidelity, there is a sense of commitment to each other. Without them, we are only infatuated with one another, and our love is short-lived. It is crucial to renew your love for each other daily. If it is not, you will quickly become objects in passing and never connected to each other. Show your love and commitment to your partner not with lip service but let it be demonstrated through your actions.

Personal Reflection
How can I apply this passage of scripture and nugget to my marriage?

_____

_____

_____

_____

_____

_____

_____

Day 199

I have chosen the way of faithfulness; I have set my heart on your laws.
Psalms 119:30(NIV)

One of the great things God has given us as His creation is the freedom of choice. We have the ability to choose between what is fleshly and what is spiritual. Even in marriage, we can choose to be faithful to our partner. Though many situations, not always pleasant, may be presented to us in crucial times of our marriage. However, we must remain faithful to the cause of matrimony. This can only come through the renewing of your mind each day. The "ing" means that it is an ongoing process. Yes, it is a challenge, but it can be done with the help of God. The scripture says, " I have chosen the way of truth (faithfulness). Our marriage should mirror the true essence of God: an unwavering commitment to each other. Know that there are consequences for each choice that we make. Choose ye this day what your actions will be. Stay in the faithful way.

Personal Reflection
How can I keep the flame of my marriage alive and thriving?

_____

_____

_____

_____

_____

_____

Day 200

It always protects, always trusts, always hopes, always perseveres.
1 Corinthians 13:7(NIV)

One of the responsibilities of a man is to protect the woman he loves. He protects her reputation, character, and her relationship with him. His concern is for her emotionally, physically, and spiritually. He will go to whatever expense to ensure the dignity of his loved one. This can also be said of the woman as well. Love makes sure that it brings out the best in each other. Love never seeks to damage but to build up and edify. It seeks the best for each other. Because of my love for my spouse, I am always careful of those who seek to taint our love, especially identifying the hand of the enemy. When we have passion, we help to strengthen what is weak and to shield the one we love from vulnerability. It's not only our duty, but it's why we love who we love.

Personal Reflection

How can I apply this passage of scripture and nugget to my marriage?

_____

_____

_____

_____

_____

_____

_____

Day 201

For the weapons of our warfare are not carnal,
but mighty through God to the pulling down of strongholds.
2 Corinthians 10:4(KJV)

There is a saying that I like to use when it comes to conflict. It is "choose your battles." Most battles are weapons, the enemy uses to throw your marriage and your relationship off. You must choose your battles carefully not to damage what you have gained by being in love with each other. We dare not do anything that would cause an end to the covenant made between the two of you. What we must do is to protect the well-being of our spouse. If battles are to come, let your battles come from without and never within. Pray for the discernment of God that with our spiritual eyes, we can fight against the tricks and schemes of the enemy. This can only be done if we are suited up each day to face the ills that may come against us, knowing that with God, we can survive the worst of times because He is our Protector. Put your armor on!!

Personal Reflection

How do I prepare for the battles we face in our marriage?

_____

_____

_____

_____

_____

Day 202

Pray without ceasing.
1 Thessalonians 5:17(KJV)

Mark 10:9(NIV) says, "Therefore, what God has joined together let no man separate." This indicates to me that marriage and the covenant of marriage will always be under attack. It also says we must always be on the defense as we stand together to protect each other. This is a challenging task, and it takes much prayer for both soul mates. The Bible also tells us that we ought to always pray, that it is a necessary part of our Christian life and marriage. Prayer is your connection to God. It is your support system when everything else fails. When you are in a relationship together with Him, there is nothing that you can't do. The Word confirms this when it says, if two of you touch and agree on earth concerning anything, it is done. Remember, this is contingent upon the depth of your relationship with Him. You must make prayer an essential part of your lives together. When this is done, watch God move!

Personal Reflection
How can I apply prayer as an essential element to the survival of my marriage?

_____

_____

_____

_____

_____

Day 203

Wherefore take unto you the whole armour of God,
that ye may be able to withstand in the evil day, and having done all, to stand.
Ephesians 6:13(KJV)

When it comes to fighting battles, we can always know that some battles are not for us to fight. If God ordained marriage, He will keep His promise that what He has joined together, no man can put asunder. When the battle is yours to fight, ensure you are fully armored. You must protect love. If you can stand on anything, stand on the Word of God. Sometimes, you must speak to the battle and stand still and see God fight it for you.

Personal Reflection

How can I apply this passage of scripture and nugget to my marriage?

_____

_____

_____

_____

_____

_____

_____

Day 204

So, teach us to number our days, that we may apply our hearts unto wisdom.
Psalms 90:12(KJV)

It is very easy to allow distractions and other events in our lives to steer us away from our spouses and our families. If our marriage and families are dear to us, we will do what is necessary to spend QT (quality time) with the ones we love. During our everyday lives, we are bombarded with many things and spirits that may take the focus away from the family. When we come home, there is no time for our spouse or families; we want "me" time. This is not good and will lead to a separation in your love for your mate and family.

Quality time for the ones we love is precious and necessary. It is a period of affirmation for those you love. Nothing you do during your day should deter you from what is needed daily to maintain a healthy family and marriage. When there is no time, MAKE TIME! Make your loved one's part of your schedule. You will find that it will open communication with your spouse and your children. Living in times like these, we cannot afford to lose our marriages or families to those things that will eventually separate us. For those of us in ministry, know that your family is important to you. We must remember that our first ministry is family.

Personal Reflection
How can I make my marriage my first ministry?

_____

_____

_____

_____

_____

_____

_____

_____

_____

_____

_____

Personal Reflection

How can I apply this passage of scripture and nugget to my marriage?

_____

_____

_____

_____

_____

_____

Day 205

That is, that I may be comforted together with you
by the mutual faith, both of you and me.
Romans 1:12(KJV)

When you decide that you are going to marry, you will soon know who your friends are. You will find the mindset of your friends will change once you are married. In fact, your spouse now becomes your best friend. Although you have other friends, you will find that there are some things sacred to the marriage. They can only be shared with the one who will be your lover for life. Your priority now is your best friend.

I am blessed to say that I am married to my best friend. Being friends is important to your marriage. Friends consider everything about you. They don't hurt each other. They are always concerned about the well-being of their friend. One of the most significant components of a successful marriage is having someone you can pour your heart out to, who will accept you and wouldn't mind being honest with you. Friendship makes the marriage stronger, fun, and it makes your communication with each other healthier. A good friendship lasts.

Personal Reflection

How is being married to my best friend an asset to our relationship?

_____

_____

_____

_____

_____

Day 206

Do not let any unwholesome talk come out of your mouths,
but what is helpful to building others up according to their needs,
that it may benefit those who listen.
Ephesians 4:29(NIV)

The Word of God calls us connected by marriage to respect and honor each other. It is our responsibility to build up and edify our mates. At no time should we take the opportunity to degrade and tear down each other. It's damaging to your relationship and your marriage. Throughout marriage, there will be times that will stretch your faith and your love for your mate, but it should NEVER take you to the point of degradation, especially in view of those outside your marriage. We all come with our defects because we aren't perfect beings. When we detect them, take them to the Creator. He knows our shortcomings and our weaknesses. We were all shaped in iniquity, but we serve a God who can fix what is broken. If you can speak a word, let it be a word that edifies. Let them know that you are grateful for them being your soul mate. Through love, serve one another. The choice is yours.

Personal Reflection

How can I better serve my spouse and seek to build them up?

_____

_____

_____

_____

_____

Day 207

There hath no temptation taken you but such as is common to man: but God is faithful, who will not suffer you to be tempted above that ye are able; but will with the temptation also make a way to escape, that ye may be able to bear it.
1 Corinthians 10:13(KJV)

Anything that can cause your marriage and your spouse displeasure should be discarded as quickly as possible. If you are not careful, bad habits, nasty dispositions, addictions, and other secrets can cause your marriage or relationship to spiral downward. It will spread like cancer and will eventually end in death. Nothing is more devastating than to have these things destroy the trust that is so needed by each of you. If anything holds you in bondage or hostage, seek God for deliverance. It might be a good idea to share these with your partner. You will need them to be your support system, and it is a great start to being honest with each other. Shake whatever it is that binds you. You will feel better when He sets you free; for whom He sets free is free indeed.

Personal Reflection
How am I working to improve myself, and seek my spouse's help?

_____

_____

_____

_____

_____

_____

Day 208

Brothers and sisters, I do not consider myself yet to have taken hold of it. But one thing I do: Forgetting what is behind and straining toward what is ahead.
Philippians 3:13(NIV)

A parasite is anything attached to you that prevents you from what you were purposed for. It drains you of energy and leaves you in bondage. They may not always include habits or things; they may also consist of people. Some of us are plagued by people we have carried into our marriages: mamas, daddies, old relationships, and close friends. Remember that we must LEAVE and CLEAVE. This means leaving those things behind and focusing on your relationship with your spouse. It can't be done if you are bound by those things that will hurt your chances for a successful marriage. Free yourself and let the main thing be the main thing.

Personal Reflection
How can I apply this passage of scripture and nugget to my marriage?

_____

_____

_____

_____

_____

_____

Day 209

The wise woman builds her house,
but with her own hands the foolish one tears hers down.
Proverbs 14:1(NIV)

In our Christian walk, we are encouraged to renew our minds by transformation. That means that we guide our minds from things detrimental to our marriage. Never measure your husband by the standards of someone else. Know that he is unique and carefully crafted by God. You must never stop being his greatest support system. If there is encouragement or image building, it should start at home. Steer away from TV shows and reality TV that give poor examples of what marriages and relationships are built upon. If you wish to find good examples of marriage and great examples of virtuous women, you can find them all over the Bible. You must strive to build your marriage on a foundation where God is the contractor. Seek Him in all that pertains to your husband and your family. Unless He builds the house, your work will be for naught. That's wisdom.

Personal Reflection

How am I centering the foundation of my marriage around God?

_____

_____

_____

_____

_____

_____

Day 210

But understand this: If the owner of the house had known at what time
of night the thief was coming, he would have kept watch and
would not have let his house be broken into.
Matthew 24:43(NIV)

Being head of your household is serious business. It is a responsibility that every man should consider when taking on a wife and a family. God has commanded man to leave his father and mother to cleave to a wife who he will now become her sole supporter. As He is the Head of the Church, so is man the head of his household. It is now vital for all husbands to take their position in the family seriously. That means developing your woman emotionally, physically, and spiritually. If you fulfill your role as husband, nothing can come between what God has joined together. Because you are a godly man, you will stick with your mate through all kinds of weather, good or bad. Take your responsibility with a deep sense of commitment. You owe it to your spouse.

Personal Reflection
How can I apply this passage of scripture and nugget to my marriage?

_____

_____

_____

_____

_____

_____

Day 211

The world and its desires pass away, but whoever does the will of God lives forever.
1 John 2:17(NIV)

An actual accomplishment of a good marriage is a marriage that's in the will of God. Staying true to your vow's commitment is essential to your marriage. There will be distractions, temptations, and stumbling blocks that will deter us from our true purpose. Our desire should always be to be intertwined with the will of God. In His will, we will always desire to bring Him glory. For us to know His will, we must first know Him. Be sure that whatever you do in your marriage, you pray to God for direction. When we operate outside of His will, we can be sure that our plans will surely fail. Allow Him to guide your way. In everything you do, consult God, and He will give you clear directions.

Personal Reflection
How am I striving to live my life and operate in the will of God?

_____

_____

_____

_____

_____

_____

Day 212

Blessed is the man that walketh not in the counsel of the ungodly, nor standeth in the way of sinners, nor sitteth in seat of the scornful. But his delight is in the law of the Lord; and in his law doth he meditate day and night.
Psalms 1:1-2(KJV)

Never allow the lust of your eyes or the loyalty of your heart to be distracted by anything or anyone. There are adverse effects that will look good to you and cause your eyes and heart to wander. Remember, the grass is not always greener on the other side; it's deceiving. We should spend our time and energies doing whatever is necessary to keep the marriage alive, fun, and enriching. If it is not maintained, you will find your mind straying. Make every effort to sustain your marriage by staying intimate with each other and keeping the fire burning. For that to be done, you've got to keep adding to the fire.

Personal Reflection
What am I doing to keep my marriage alive and fun?

_____

_____

_____

_____

_____

_____

_____

Day 213

No, in all these things we are more than conquerors through Him that loved us.
Romans 8:37(NIV)

1 John 2:16 tells us not to get infatuated with the things of this world; they are only temporal and will pass away. Those people, places, or things that you wet your taste buds will eventually lead to your destruction and interfere with our relationships. The lust of the eyes is the desire to have the things we see. Those worldly passions separate us from our spouses and cause us to lose focus of what we vowed to do: to love each other no matter what. With the aid of the Holy Spirit, we can recognize the traps and tricks of the enemy and remain committed to our marriages. Remember that Jesus conquered every temptation placed before Him. We are more than conquerors through Him. We can only survive worldly lusts and pleasures by remaining connected to Him. You will never make it without Him. Without God, we can do nothing; without Him, we will surely fail.

Personal Reflection
How can I apply this passage of scripture and nugget to my marriage?

_____

_____

_____

_____

_____

Day 214

What causes fights and quarrels among you?
Don't they come from your desires that battle within you?
James 4:1(NIV)

All through life, we are faced with those things that distract us and look good to the natural eye. It's like candy that we have to have. This is deceptive and could lead to many things that can take us to a point of no return. What looks good to us is not always good for us. It is important for us to be connected to our spouses. What we should do is to make sure that every need of our spouse is met. When there is a lack and that need is not met, there is always the deceptive spirit of the enemy to present them with what looks good through the eyes of lust. Know that with lust comes a horrific price.

Jesus Himself endured the lust presented to Him in Matthew 4. Satan tried every trick he could to attack Jesus at His weakest point. Jesus demonstrated that we can endure them, but we've got to be armed. With what? Notice that He uses the Word to counteract every enemy attack; It is written. This is a powerful spirit! The world is full of visuals that are pleasing to us, materialistic gains, power, position, and self-fulfillment. Our focus should be on our marriages and not those things that distract us from our spouses. We should all know what we're dealing with and keep our eyes on Jesus.

Personal Reflection
How am I building myself to refrain from material and physical lust?

_____

_____

_____

_____

_____

_____

_____

_____

_____

_____

Personal Reflection
How can I apply this passage of scripture and nugget to my marriage?

_____

_____

_____

_____

_____

_____

_____

_____

Day 215

The one who calls you is faithful, and He will do it.
1 Thessalonians 5:24(NIV)

During your relationship or marriage, you will receive warning signs alerting that some things have become inoperative. When this occurs, you must take a quick self-assessment of yourself and the direction in which your marriage is going. Distractions can quickly steer us from what we think is better for us but will soon prove fatal. It's like checking your car periodically for possible repairs and upgrades. Do I have enough gas to get there? Is it time for servicing? Am I in need of a tune-up? If you are not assessing your marriage and relationship, you will find that it will run out of gas and need servicing. Lust and other worldly distractions will make you think you need to trade. Stay focused! Spend quality time validating your love for each other. Never let a day go by that you are not focusing on preserving your marriage. Nothing is more important than my relationship with my lover for life. Both of us must do what we must to remain faithful and loyal to the marriage covenant.

Personal Reflection

How am I periodically assessing and evaluating the course of my marriage?

_____

_____

_____

_____

_____

_____

_____

_____

_____

_____

_____

Personal Reflection
How can I apply this passage of scripture and nugget to my marriage?

_____

_____

_____

_____

_____

_____

_____

_____

_____

Day 216

*His divine power has given us everything we need for a godly life
through our knowledge of him who called us by his own glory and
goodness. Through these he has given us his very great and precious promises,
so that through them you may participate in the divine nature,
having escaped the corruption in the world caused by evil desires.*
2 Peter 1:3-4(NIV)

When your eyes are on Jesus, you can be consistent in your love for your spouse. Everything is centered around pleasing Him and bringing Him glory. So, with your marriage, your commitment to each other is the center of your attention. When I am in tune with my spouse, I am careful not to be swayed by the distractions and affection of others. Focus on Him and stay prayerful about those things that may come against you and your spouse. God has promised that what He has joined together, nothing would separate. That means you must know He will fight your battles when you are attacked. Remember what the Word of God says: If God be for us, who can be against us?

Personal Reflection
How can I apply this passage of scripture and nugget to my marriage?

_____

_____

_____

_____

_____

Day 217

As for God, His way is perfect: The Lord's Word is flawless;
He shields all who take refuge in Him.
Psalms 18:30(NIV)

The Word of God is powerful. It is the unfailing promises of God to those whom He loves. Our only hope to capitalize on the promises that He has made is to know what the promises are. We miss so much of what God has promised because we don't know what they are. The Bible says, "Faith comes by hearing, and hearing by the Word of God." If we set our eyes on His Word by digesting it daily, we can speak to situations and circumstances in our life. You can speak to the enemy as he tries to infiltrate your marriage. If you know the Word of God, you can speak peace when the storms of life are raging. Stay in the Word.

Personal Reflection
How am I applying the Word of God to my marriage?

_____

_____

_____

_____

_____

_____

Day 218

Give thanks in all circumstances; for this is God's will for you in Christ Jesus.
1 Thessalonians 5:18(NIV)

Marriage comes with its many challenges. While sharing life, we will share many experiences that will help shape us as individuals and as a couple. It is the attitude that we take that will determine how we handle what we experience. The Bible tells us that we should be thankful in everything, knowing that what we experience together will help us to become one. Every trial and every test are parts of our process as a couple. We can show God our gratitude by praising Him through it all, knowing that it will work out for our good. Our attitudes will affect our altitude.

Personal Reflection
How can I apply this passage of scripture and nugget to my marriage?

_____

_____

_____

_____

_____

_____

Day 219

May your fountain be blessed, and may you rejoice in the wife of your youth.
A loving doe, a graceful deer may her breasts satisfy you always,
may you ever be intoxicated with her love.
Why, my son, be intoxicated with another man's wife?
Why embrace the bosom of a wayward woman?
For your ways are in full view of the Lord, and he examines all your paths.
Proverbs 5:18-21(NIV)

You should always treat your marriage like your job. There is always work to do to maintain your relationship with your spouse. If your focus is on your mate, there is never room to look elsewhere. Do all you can to keep the marriage thriving with much love, fun, and intimacy. When it becomes dull it falls victim to everything that will lead to the destruction of your level of intimacy. If your marriage is successful, it is because both of you chose to go that extra mile to do what is necessary to keep your marriage alive. Find out what the needs of your partner are and make them happen. It will help make your marriage successful and eliminate any distress. It is work that is ongoing; it never stops.

Personal Reflection
How can I apply this passage of scripture and nugget to my marriage?

_____

_____

_____

_____

_____

Day 220

Do not love the world or anything in the world.
If anyone loves the world, love for the Father is not in them.
1 John 2:15(NIV)

The desire of a marriage should never be materialistic or lustful for the things of this world. Everything in this life is temporal and not lasting. Our first desire should be to love God with all we have knowing that He can supply us with ALL we need. When we love God, we can better be able to love each other and appreciate everything about each other. This includes the good, bad, or indifferent. It's really about Him; if we seek His godly principles first, all that we need and desire will be added to us. In order for any marriage to be successful, God must be first. He can provide you with the best life has to offer. Know that every good and perfect gift comes from Him. James 1:17 Love hard!

Personal Reflection
How am I keeping God at the center of my marriage?

_____

_____

_____

_____

_____

_____

_____

Day 221

Anyone you forgive, I also forgive. And what I have forgiven—if there was anything to forgive—I have forgiven in the sight of Christ for your sake.
2 Corinthians 2:10(NIV)

One of the most powerful practices in a marriage is forgiveness. We all know that allowing our hurt and frustrations to grow within us without bringing them to our mate's attention will lead to disaster. Holding on to past hurts can lead to resentment and cause communication issues critical to your marriage. Resolve any problems in your marriage and ask for God's help moving on. Remember that we are all susceptible to error, but we must never let that affect our love for each other. If we love each other, we can look beyond many faults and failures and do what we must to maintain love and trust. Jesus has given us the greatest example: we are loved despite our shortcomings. Forgiveness is powerful; learn to use it. It can help to bring healing to your relationship.

Personal Reflection
How am I in the area of forgiveness? Is forgiveness hard for me?

_____

_____

_____

_____

_____

_____

Day 222

And when you stand praying, if you hold anything against anyone,
forgive them so that your Father in Heaven may forgive you your sins.
Mark 11:25(NIV)

Jesus had a very important discussion on forgiveness in Matthew 18:21-25. The question is asked as to how many times should one forgive. Jesus answered that it's done as often as needed, without hesitation or reservation. He tells the story of a servant who was forgiven by the king but couldn't find it in his heart to forgive others. Forgiveness is like a boomerang. It can come back to haunt you if not handled appropriately. Forgiveness should be limitless. It will free you of the hurt, bitterness, and resentment eating at you. With this freedom comes the restoration and healing of your relationship. Your marriage will not survive without it! It's a choice we must make in loving others, especially our spouses, as Christ loves us.

Personal Reflection
How can I apply this passage of scripture and nugget to my marriage?

_____

_____

_____

_____

_____

_____

Day 223

This is how my heavenly Father will treat each of you,
unless you forgive your brother or sister from your heart.
Matthew 18:35(NIV)

Unforgiveness is a crippler to your relationship and smothers you of every effort to have a successful marriage. You should know that nothing you petition God for is answered if you have an unforgiving spirit. Unforgiveness distorts your communication and connection to God. He has said in His Word that if we can't forgive, He won't forgive us. It delays every blessing and promise He has made to you. What is vital in this process is that you forgive and move on. Don't be handcuffed to what can cause you emotional and spiritual complications. Give it to the one who can first deal with you from the inside out and allow you with His spirit to forgive. Is it easy? I don't think so, but it is the start of healing your soul. Do you need to forgive your spouse today? Don't put the one you love through a bitter and resentful relationship. Didn't you say you'd loved them through it all?

Personal Reflection
How can I apply this passage of scripture and nugget to my marriage?

_____

_____

_____

_____

_____

_____

Day 224

And do not be conformed to this world,
but be transformed by the renewing of your mind,
that you may prove what is that good and acceptable and perfect will of God.
Romans 12:2(NKJV)

It's about freedom. It's about letting go. With forgiveness comes a period of change. It is when the one being forgiven must make a concerted effort not to repeat the same mistake. It will lead to distrust and eventually taint your relationship with each other. There must be conditions established to ensure that what has caused a rift in the marriage is addressed. This may include fasting and praying to heal the hurt and destroy what has caused the damage. What can be a stumbling block would be the constant rehashing of the fault and never really dealing with the problem. When we've forgiven someone, we have turned it over to God and asked Him to give us what we need to love again despite the hurt it has caused. Renew your mind daily to free yourself from being held hostage to those things that have hurt you. This can only take place when you've indeed given it to God.

Personal Reflection

Do I hold on to old issues? How can I continue to work on forgiveness?

_____

_____

_____

_____

_____

Day 225

Bear with each other and forgive one another
if any of you has a grievance against someone.
Forgive as the Lord forgave you.
Colossians 3:13(NIV)

Forgiveness is a matter of choice; you can choose to let it consume you, or you can forgive and move on. It does not leave us to feel that the act committed against us doesn't hurt and cause us some discomfort, nor does it justify it. What it does is lead us to a path of peace. Frustration, anxiety, resentment, and anger can lead to physical and emotional problems. We must ask for a peace that only God can give; it surpasses our understanding. Don't become a victim because you can't forgive, but become a victor because He has given you power over the situation, and you are now on your way to spiritual healing.

Personal Reflection
How can I apply this passage of scripture and nugget to my marriage?

_____

_____

_____

_____

_____

_____

Day 226

Do not take revenge, my dear friends, but leave room for God's wrath,
for it is written: "It is mine to avenge; I will repay," says the Lord.
Romans 12:19(NIV)

There are many times when we stick our noses into things that we can't do anything about. We become judge, jury, and executioner to those things or situations that involve us. We want it to be punitive to what we deem is suitable for the offense. Know that it's outside your job description, and you will never have the final word. It all belongs to God, and we should learn to leave it there. Spend that time working on forgiveness and healing. Work on the forgiveness process together if you are in a relationship or marriage. Discuss the hurt it has caused, but also be in the spirit of forgiving. This will help both of you deal with the situation so that it will never again knock at your door. Discuss your expectations and what the both of you will do to prevent further heartache. Only do this by praying to the Lord for direction and the healing process. You can't make it without Him.

Personal Reflection

What can I do as a spouse to help to prevent discord and conflict in my marriage?

_____

_____

_____

_____

_____

_____

Day 227

Offer hospitality to one another without grumbling.
1 Peter 4:9(NIV)

Love is a strange phenomenon. It does things that may not make sense to us. When we have been wronged, especially by the one we love, love forgives. True love will allow you to trust God in all painful situations and never look back. Now, this can be challenging. That's why love is practiced each day of our lives. It is not confined to mere words but is demonstrated in our acts. When we took on this journey of marriage, we discovered in the process that we had to love through some things. Some unpleasant and some that could lead to the destruction of our relationship, but it's in the process that we are developed as a couple that can face life's struggles and move on. When I say love hard, I talk about reaching beyond the break. It resembles the love God has for us in that He can love us despite all of our mess. It results in a message that can be shared with others that you will go to the distance to make things work. Someone said, "it's birthed out of the affliction of painful loss. It's all about relationships. Let it go and make it work.

Personal Reflection

What can I do to continuously work at making our marriage work?

_____

_____

_____

_____

_____

Day 228

You, therefore, have no excuse, you who pass judgment on someone else,
for at whatever point you judge another, you are condemning yourself,
because you who pass judgment do the same things.
Romans 2:1(NIV)

There are a few lyrics in the song made famous by Michael Jackson - "Man in the Mirror." It speaks to judgment and how it starts with you & I. Before we can pass judgment on anyone, we must first examine ourselves. Let's remember that we are working with imperfection, which means there are flaws in all of us. The danger is that it can serve as a boomerang and backfire. The Bible tells us that before we can play judge and jury, we must first put the mirror on us and examine ourselves. The change starts in each of us individually. Your partner for life needs you to have the type of love that is not judgmental but in a spirit of understanding. Once we take a serious look at each other, we will find that we are all similar in nature and in the process of becoming, which God has purposed our marriage to be.

Personal Reflection

How can I examine myself and work on areas that affect my marriage?

_____

_____

_____

_____

_____

Day 229

*Be careful for nothing; but in everything by prayer and supplication
with thanksgiving let your requests be made known unto God.
Philippians 4:6(KJV)*

Go back and reminisce about how you both felt about each other. When we were dating, we were happy when we were the center of attention; it was the me syndrome. I like how you make me feel. I like what you do for me. That was before you were married. What about now? Do you still have that selfish desire that it's all about me and my wants and desires? I loved my spouse and what they did for me. In marriage, we must sometimes take the back seat and recognize that it is not all about me. It is a series of give and take, taking the time and effort to ensure that my mate's needs are met. Make every motive a stepping stone to prove how much their happiness means to you, even if that means compromising, giving up on having things as you want them - or losing. You have yet to lose it for the cause of preserving your marriage and the love you have for your spouse. Love harder than you've ever loved before.

Personal Reflection
How can I apply this passage of scripture and nugget to my marriage?

_____

_____

_____

_____

_____

_____

Day 230

A rebuke impresses a discerning person more than a hundred lashes a fool.
Proverbs 17:10(NIV)

One of the things we fail to do in marriage is listen. Our personal agenda, wants, and desires are more important to us. Sometimes it's just good to shut up and listen. In our haste to have it our way, we may be missing something crucial to communicating and relating to each other. It's not about winning the battle but coming to a calm resolution. Listening is an art many of us in marriage have not mastered, and it can sometimes lead to serious marital debates. It's always good to hear each other out. Listening requires a sense of presence; I am attentive to what you say and feel, and it is important to me. I am not just sitting, waiting for an opportunity to score, sling blame, or degrade. Listening is a way of showing respect for each other and building your relationship. It's saying that I am interested in what you are saying to me and how it affects both of us. Next time there is an argument, make sure what is said is heard and understood.

Personal Reflection
How can I apply this passage of scripture and nugget to my marriage?

_____

_____

_____

_____

_____

Day 231

He that answers a matter before he heareth it, it is folly and shame to him.
Proverb 18:13(KJV)

Marriage is a connection, two hearts interwoven to become one. You two become the most important people in each other's lives. Your job is to ensure that your spouse's needs are met spiritually, emotionally, physically, and sexually. I read an article that stated that a man had six primary love needs: trust, respect, appreciation, admiration, approval, and encouragement. The woman needs caring, understanding, validation, respect, devotion, and reassurance. There are many others, but we must pay close attention to our spouse's needs and ask: am I meeting all my spouse's needs? This leads to the communication component. Are we articulating these shortcomings or neglecting the needs of our mates? If they are not discussed, they cannot be addressed. When we know what these needs are, we can improve our relationships. Ask your spouse today if you are fulfilling their needs. Don't get offensive, but LISTEN. It won't hurt (not long), it helps!

Personal Reflection
How am I meeting the needs of my spouse?

_____

_____

_____

_____

_____

Day 232

No, in all these things we are more than conquerors through Him who loved us.
For I am convinced that neither death nor life, neither angels nor demons,
neither the present nor the future, nor any powers, neither height nor depth,
nor anything else in all creation, will be able to separate us
from the love of God that is in Christ Jesus our Lord.
Romans 8:37-39(NIV)

I enjoy the responsibility of taking care of my spouse. It is a vow that I intend to honor until my last breath. If we look at what we do every day for each other, despite our differences at times, we stay committed to doing whatever it takes to make our relationships work. First, we must recognize that a relationship is meaningful in a marriage. It is an ongoing process that must be nurtured daily. It's like putting wood on a fire. It will eventually fade if you are not constantly remaining true to keeping the home fire burning. Many relationships are damaged because we've allowed mistakes and past hurts to consume us and cause our love for our spouse to fade. Relationship first starts with God and is transmitted to our spouses and everyone we come in contact with. If we haven't learned to love God, we will NEVER know what true love is.

If we practiced Christ's unconditional love, there would be no cause for separation and divorce. Your spouse has somehow changed and is different from when you were married. Yet, you have this persevering spirit to go all the way. I'm in it to win it. It is the same type of love God has for us, and we should make every effort to model that love with our spouses. It will become a little easier for us when we are in a relationship with God. I can't emphasize enough the importance of having God in the formula. With Him, we can do things that would blow our minds in the natural, but in the spiritual, we know that it is in Him that we can experience a life that will bring Glory to Him.

Personal Reflection
What am I doing to maintain my love and fellowship with my spouse?

_____

_____

_____

_____

_____

Personal Reflection
How has God played a role in my life and in my marriage?

_____

_____

_____

_____

_____

_____

_____

_____

Day 233

Pride goeth before destruction, and a haughty spirit before a fall.
Proverbs 16:18(KJV)

Pride is a killer; the Bible says that God despises a proud look. It binds you when it is necessary to forgive and move on. It could mean bondage to your relationship and marriage. Always examine yourself to ensure that this demonic spirit does not hurt and damage you as an individual and a husband or wife. To avoid this spirit, we must have control of our flesh because it is a natural inclination for us to give way to it. We must remember that it is through humility that we maintain a spiritual and meaningful relationship with our spouse and our fellow man. If it is not managed correctly, it can hinder any attempts for restoration and forgiveness. When you feel this spirit or are faced with it, pray to God for power to overcome it.

Personal Reflection
How can I apply humility to my marriage and free myself of pride?

_____

_____

_____

_____

_____

_____

Day 234

If we claim to be without sin, we deceive ourselves and the truth is not in us.
If we confess our sins, he is faithful and just
and will forgive us our sins and purify us from all unrighteousness.
1John 1:8-9(NIV)

We are all sinners saved by grace. Each day, God is doing what He does to conform us to the image of His Son. This means that we are in the process of becoming. One of our gifts is that we serve a forgiving God despite our flaws and shortcomings. No matter how messy we become, He is there with outstretched arms to redeem us, cleanse us, and not only give us another chance but He forgives us repeatedly. It is important in marriage that we confess our faults to God so that we can better handle the times in our process when we must be able to build on our relationships. This means that it starts with each of us individually. What areas do we need God to cover to help us overcome or cut from our lives? Allow it to begin with you! Is it your pride, arrogance, your unwillingness to compromise? Any sin that inhibits you from developing a loving and lasting relationship with your lover must go. Ask God today to remove anything that separates you from Him and then you and your spouse.

Personal Reflection
How can I apply this passage of scripture and nugget to my marriage?

_____

_____

_____

_____

Day 235

Be angry, and do not sin, do not let the sun go down on your wrath.
Ephesians 4:26(NKJV)

Have you ever picked up your phone and heard static on the line? There needed to be a better connection, and you couldn't communicate well with the person you were calling. When we are out of God's will or have been overtaken by sin, our connection to God is off. Sin separates us from Him. We have to make a conscious effort each day to be sure that we are in good standing with our Creator. If there is a wrong place to be, it is out of the will and favor of God. When we are, we are unable to hear Him speak to us clearly; it separates us from Him. Confess your faults before Him. He will be faithful to His Word and forgive you. The same is to be said about your marriage. Never let a day go by that you are separated from your lover because of fault or periods of non-communication. Get it right! It isn't worth the fight or the sleepless nights. Promise yourself and your spouse that you will NEVER close your eyes at night until you have brought any disagreements or strife to closure. Forgive and move on.

Personal Reflection

How am I working with my spouse to keep our communication open and free of finger-pointing?

_____

_____

_____

_____

_____

Day 236

Get rid of all bitterness, rage and anger, brawling and slander,
along with every form of malice. Be kind and compassionate to one another,
forgiving each other, just as in Christ forgave you.
Ephesians 4:31-32(NIV)

Many unresolved issues may occur in your marriage. These issues can be cancer and eventually spread to other areas of your marriage. Even when marriages have existed for an extended period, there are still times when unresolved issues may cause much grief and stress. Be swift in the resolution of conflict. Admit to your wrongdoings and ask for the forgiveness of your mate. If you love your spouse, your love for each other will erase the offense and bring healing to both of you. However, when the issue has been resolved, never let it arise again in conversation, such as refusing to forgive past hurts. When we remember that we are both imperfect beings, capable of mistakes and error, we can best accept each other as individuals.

Personal Reflection
How can I apply this nugget to solving conflict in my marriage?

_____

_____

_____

_____

_____

_____

Day 237

*If we confess our sins, he is faithful and just and will forgive us our sins
and purify us from all unrighteousness.*
1 John 1:9(NIV)

Admitting your faults to each other is the first step toward a good marriage. It is great to confess that you have made mistakes and be willing to share them with your spouse in a spirit of humility. It's humbling and an example of what we are to do first with our God. We already know that He remains faithful if we confess our sins or faults to Him. For some of us, this is hard because we allow so many other things to cloud our thinking: pride, arrogance, chauvinist, and stubbornness. We must first get it right with God and pray for His divine guidance when making things right with our spouses. Never let your failure to make things right hinder your marriage. Talk about it, be honest, and let God do the rest. To everything there is a season, a time to admit that you are wrong, and a time to say I'm sorry. Afford your marriage the opportunity to weather every storm. Make it right!

Personal Reflection
How can I apply this passage of scripture and nugget to my marriage?

_____

_____

_____

_____

_____

_____

Day 238

Each one should test their own actions. Then they can take pride in themselves alone, without comparing themselves to someone else.
Galatians 6:4(NIV)

We have work to do in our marriage, individually and collectively. The question is, how hard are you working to maintain your marriage, to keep it vibrant and loving? Are you continually working on yourself such that nothing within you can damage what you both have together? It starts within and works its way out. Do all you can by periodically taking a self-examination and making the necessary changes to you. Doing this will allow your marriage to remain your top priority and be what it was designed and purposed to be.

Personal Reflection
How often do we assess our marital growth and take self-examinations?

_____

_____

_____

_____

_____

_____

Day 239

Guard my life and rescue me; do not let me be put to shame, for I take refuge in you.
Psalms 25:20(NIV)

Your relationship or marriage is and will always be under attack. Those outside forces will seek to destroy what God has ordained. To keep you and your marriage grounded, you must pray for God's covering to give you the spiritual eye to see those things that seek to damage and destroy your marriage. He will guide you in all things. The Word says that the steps of a good man/woman are ordered by the Lord. Know that you can't be under any better protection than safe in the arms of Jesus. It's a protection you can trust.

Personal Reflection
How can I apply this passage of scripture and nugget to my marriage?

_____

_____

_____

_____

_____

_____

Day 240

Trust in the Lord with all thine heart; and lean not unto thine own understanding.
In all thy ways acknowledge Him and He shall direct your path.
Proverbs 3:5-6(KJV)

Our view of marriage today is skewed by what we envision marriage to be in our minds. We have this mental picture of what we want our mate to be like and how we want to live happily ever after. The reality is that marriage is so much more than that. That's why it is important for those contemplating marriage to seek God for His divine direction. The merging of two personalities requires much prayer and work. If we enter marriage without knowing what it entails, it will most times end in disarray. For those of us who are already on the marriage trail, we have found that it takes adjustments on both parties. It requires a new mindset: us versus me. We have the understanding that we are first individuals and then we are a couple. We may never think the same, but we learn to appreciate and live with our differences. In our Christian walk, we are constantly transforming; that means we are renewing our thinking. In this process, our hopes and dreams as a couple are realized.

Personal Reflection
How am I transforming my mind to adjust to our personality differences?

_____

_____

_____

_____

_____

Day 241

I will praise thee for I am fearfully and wonderfully made:
Marvelous are thou works,
and that my soul knoweth right well.
Psalms 139:14(KJV)

It isn't easy to go through life living by the expectations of others. In a way, this could be miserable. You will never be allowed to be who God created you to be - unique. That's the joy of having a spouse or mate. You enjoy the individuality that each of you brings to your marriage. I tried once to change who my wife was, but I had to realize I had to allow her to be who she was. Once I did that, I discovered that we had attributes that complimented each other. It's not in us to change anyone. When we have things that don't fit, don't work, not what we want, what do we do? We return them to the manufacturer or the store we bought them from. God is the Creator, designer, and orchestrator. Only He can intervene and fix what is broken. Give it to Him and leave it there.

Personal Reflection
How can I apply this passage of scripture and nugget my marriage?

_____

_____

_____

_____

_____

_____

Day 242

How can you say to your brother, let me take the speck out of your eye,
when all the time there is a plank in your own eye?
You hypocrite, first take the plank out of your own eye,
and then you will see clearly to remove the speck from your brother's eye.
Matthew 7:4-5(NIV)

Each year, we make appointments with our physicians for our annual check-ups to see where we are physically. If something is out of whack, he will either give us a prescription or give suggestions to correct it. When we make these adjustments, we will either feel a little better or make it our business to change our lifestyles, whether it be our diet or way of work. It's our responsibility to take the opportunity daily not to examine the lives and business of others but us. There is a gospel song that says "Sweep around your own front door." Take the time to look in the mirror and examine yourself. Make every attempt to work on self-improvement and do your best to be a good wife or husband. If you let your light shine, your spouse may take the time to start examining themselves.

Personal Reflection
What am I doing for self-improvement to be the best spouse I can be?

_____

_____

_____

_____

_____

Day 243

Do not conform to the pattern of this world, but be transformed by the renewing of your mind. Then you will be able to test and approve what God's will is—his good, pleasing and perfect will.
Romans 12:2(NIV)

There are only two constants in life: God and change. We can look back over our lives and should see a change in us and our spouse. If there is no change, something is definitely wrong. There should always be a challenge in your marriage to improve things for you and each other. It's not about control but about working this thing out together. It starts in our thinking, and it is where the change begins. When you awaken each morning, you can decide your attire for that day. You have control over what you will grace the world with that day. If you need to be in control of things in life and around you, start with your mind; it is in your control. There should be a renewing of the mind taking place every day, seeking to change.

Personal Reflection

How have I changed me, and how I can effectively control my life?

_____

_____

_____

_____

_____

_____

Day 244

Therefore, shall a man leave his father and his mother,
and shall cleave unto his wife: and they shall become one flesh.
Genesis 2:24(KJV)

In marriage, we learn to nurture each other. The home is your safe haven, where you can have the freedom of expression and not be a target of judgment. We are free to be who we are!! Marriage is not dull, it's something that's watered every moment of your time together. When we spend that quality time making sure that we are first comfortable with ourselves and then making sure that we are fulfilling our roles as a spouse. That's why it is important to leave and cleave.

It is part of being one flesh. Two hearts, two personalities interwoven into what could be a journey of happiness. We have a God-given responsibility to love and serve our spouse. To do that, we must love effectively by knowing every minute detail: faults, failures, likes, dislikes. It comes with the territory. If you have spent the time discovering the deep intimate details of your spouse, you will have the staying power that will keep you for better and worse.

Personal Reflection
How can I apply this passage of scripture and nugget to my marriage?

_____

_____

_____

_____

Day 245

Therefore encourage one another and build each other up, just as in fact you are doing.
1 Thessalonians 5:11(NIV)

The greatest boost that we can get from anyone is to get it from the one we love. If I expect anyone to be my number one fan, it's the one I love. Someone who should never put me down but is there to inspire and push me to my highest level of achievement. Even when I fall short, they are there to pick me up and encourage me to go on. We vow to do that for each other. During the course of our love life, we learn to love each other in spite of our differences. Never is there a day that we would not want the best for our spouse. Every day, we are building on our relationship by being each other's support system. We are no longer two but one. My success is her success, and her success is mine. We take joy in the successes and failures of each other, knowing that we're in it to win it. Come hell or high water, we remain committed to each other through it all.

Personal Reflection
How can I best support my spouse and contribute to their success?

_____

_____

_____

_____

_____

_____

Day 246

For you created my inmost being; you knit me together in my mother's womb.
I praise you because I am fearfully and wonderfully made;
your works are wonderful, I know that full well.
Psalms 139:13-14(NIV)

Each of us needs to realize who God purposed us to be. What is unique about the creation process is that God made each of us unique. There are no two people with the same makeup. That's why it is vital that we align ourselves with the will of God to be what he has purposed us to be. When we try to be who we are not, we are nothing but imitators of what someone else expects us to be. The only expectation we should live up to is that of our Creator. Don't put your spouse in bondage, by trying to shape them to your expectations. Who are you? Allow them to be who they were created to be. The rest is up to God to fulfill His purpose in their lives. What you can do is appreciate what they bring to the marriage and how, through your bonding, you will discover a new-found appreciation for them.

Personal Reflection
How can I apply this passage of scripture and nugget to my marriage?

_____

_____

_____

_____

_____

_____

Day 247

And let us consider how we may spur one another on toward love and good deeds.
Hebrews 10:24(NIV)

Enjoyment and happiness come from an ongoing process of doing those things that make your partner happy. It's as simple as doing something even when you are not asked. What can you do today that will add that extra spice to your spouse's day? A reminder to them via email that you are still in love with them, a spontaneous drop-in at work to take them out to lunch, a "me" day when you take on all the chores, including feeding the children and helping them with homework. Love is not selfish. It is doing what is necessary to make your spouse feel loved and appreciated.

Personal Reflection
How can I apply this nugget to add that special touch to my marriage?

_____

_____

_____

_____

_____

_____

Day 248

Bless the Lord O my soul, and forget not all His benefits.
Psalms 103:2(NKJV)

Never consider your marriage and your commitment to your spouse as a duty. Your marriage is a ministry, one that God Himself sanctioned. Because He has ordained it, He is the only one able to help you sustain and maintain it. Every day is an opportunity for both of you to lift your marriage to Him, asking God to make a difference in each of you. Pray that He gives you the know-how to love in adverse times and that you love each other unconditionally. For those of us who have withstood the best of times, take the opportunity this today to thank God for how He has kept you through it all. To the new couple, pray for His divine hand in every area of your life together as husband and wife. He is the glue that holds this world together, and how much more will He do to keep you committed to the vow between the two of you?

Personal Reflection
How can I apply this passage of scripture and nugget to my marriage?

_____

_____

_____

_____

_____

_____

Day 249

As iron sharpens iron, so one person sharpens another.
Proverbs 27:17(NIV)

And the two become one flesh. What does that mean to you? In the course of marriage, a connection occurs because there is so much shared between the two of you. In the process, you will learn everything there is to know about your mate: the highs and the lows, the ins and outs. Sometimes, we must shield our mates from everything that will cause them harm or hurt. We should be able to sense those moments when they are experiencing troubled times. Be observant and sensitive to those times in the life of your spouse. It is essential for us to soften the blow and to be the one that helps to carry the load. When we are sensitive to each other's needs, we are more able to bond with each other. It requires time, energy, and commitment from both of you. Take the time to notice your spouse. This means observing the signs they give you through conversation and demeanor. Where do you stand in knowing what you need to know about your spouse?

Personal Reflection

How can I protect my spouse from those outside sources that may affect them and our bond?

_____

_____

_____

_____

_____

_____

Day 250

Perfume and incense bring joy to the heart,
and the pleasantness of a friend springs from their heartfelt advice.
Proverbs 27:9(NIV)

One of the most treasured elements of a marriage is the quality of friendship between the two of you. The quality of that friendship is how well you know each other. Being a friend means taking the necessary time to understand every intimate detail. With that friendship grows a love that responds to every moment of your lives together. Your love for your spouse is more than living in the same house or sleeping in the same bed. It knows their dreams, ambitions, wants, dislikes, and desires. It's more than being interested in what they can give you or what they bring to the marriage: a good salary, material things, or worldly possessions. These things will perish and become non-existent, but love will last when my interest lies in the happiness of the one I have decided to spend my life with. Take the time today to invest in your spouse by sacrificing to be in tune with them.

Personal Reflection
How can I apply this passage of scripture and nugget to my marriage?

_____

_____

_____

_____

_____

Day 251

We are hard pressed on every side, but not crushed; perplexed, but not in despair;
persecuted, but not abandoned; struck down, but not destroyed.
2 Corinthians 4:8-9(NIV)

How often do we come home in the evenings stressed with the toils and cares of the day? Our spouses often fall victim to our day that they haven't contributed to. We must never allow it to follow us to the place that is supposed to be stress-free. Leave it at the gate!! Stress is contagious; don't let it ride with you! On your ride home, start praying for God to give you that peace that passes all understanding, that you will enter your home with an attitude of I can find peace here. If you detect that stress is written all over your mate, pull out all of the stops to relieve them of whatever frustrations they may be feeling.

Sometimes, it is just listening to what they've experienced without giving advice. Many times, it is just being that sounding board for them. Never be in the mindset that you never want to hear about the things that stress them. If you love them, you are concerned about what affects them. Spend that time comforting them by doing those things that could be stress relievers: back or foot massage, exercising together, a good swim, and even lovemaking. It is important to devise a plan so that each of you can support each other in times of stress.

Personal Reflection
How do you effectively hear the heart of my spouse?

_____

_____

_____

_____

Day 252

For I was hungry and you gave me something to eat, I was thirsty and you gave me something to drink, I was a stranger and you invited me in, I needed clothes and you clothed me, I was sick and you looked after me, I was in prison and you came to visit me.
Matthew 25:35-40(NIV)

One of the attributes of a giver is that they are never concerned about themselves but about the well-being of others. Love is not selfish, but it aims to please the one you love; always remember that what is given will return to you. Scripture tells us that love is kind, which means that selfishness does not fit into the actions of love. In marriage, we operate with the mindset that the interest of our spouse is important to us. Philippians 2:3(NIV) states "Do nothing out of selfish or vain conceit. Rather, in humility, value others above yourselves". How can you demonstrate an act of kindness to your mate today? Whatever it is, do it.

Personal Reflection
How can I demonstrate my love and appreciation to my lover for life?

_____

_____

_____

_____

_____

_____

Day 253

Continue to love deeply.
Then make my joy complete by being like-minded,
having the same love, being one in spirit and of one mind.
Philippians 2:2(NIV)

True love runs deep; it goes to the limit for the one on the receiving end. It bears all things, hopes all things, endures all things. Love will do what is necessary to meet the needs of the one being loved. This is as simple as a pleasant and understanding heart that will be there for their spouse in the good and bad times. Marriage is full of sacrifices. It keeps us in touch with what is important: the well-being of the one we love. It is truly worth the sacrifice. It resembles Christ's sacrifice when He sacrifices His life for us.

Personal Reflection

What is important to me and the success of my marriage?

_____

_____

_____

_____

_____

_____

Day 254

Husbands, in the same way be considerate as you live with your wives, and treat them with respect as the weaker partner and as heir with you of the gracious gift of life, so that nothing will hinder your prayers.
1 Peter 3:7(NIV)

What is essential to marriage is the concessions and extra things that you do for each other. We must do whatever is needed to make our spouses happy by going over and beyond to do it. We must acknowledge our commitment to each other to make those sacrifices for each other. Are we in it for the long haul, and how deep is our investment in our lives together? Sometimes, our sacrifices will force us to give up those things we do for our partner's good. If we see that our time together is important, we make accommodations to make it happen. Sacrificing is working together as a couple to find those things that will work better for both of you. It is a willingness to shift our wants and desires to our spouse.

Personal Reflection
How committed am I to the longevity of my love and relationship with my spouse?

_____

_____

_____

_____

_____

_____

Day 255

And this is my prayer: that your love may abound more and more in knowledge and depth of insight, 10 so that you may be able to discern what is best and may be pure and blameless for the day of Christ.
Philippians 1:9-10(NIV)

Our first obligation to our lovers for life is to love them with all we have. To make a sacrifice for them is giving up something that's important to you. It could be giving up the football game or that Friday evening to make it a special evening for the one you love. Sacrifice comes with some drawbacks. When you sacrifice, it is not selfish or thoughtless, but it's giving oneself to the good of the marriage. Sacrifice directly impacts your relationship with your spouse, giving up your comforts for the sake of others. Jesus gave up His royalty to be a ransom for us, to show us how much we meant to Him. But God demonstrates His love for us in that Christ died for us while we were still sinners (Romans 5:8). That was the ultimate sacrifice. How much are you willing to sacrifice for your marriage and your spouse?

Personal Reflection
How can I apply this passage of scripture and nugget to my marriage?

_____

_____

_____

_____

_____

Day 256

Carry each other's burdens, and in this way, you will fulfill the law of Christ.
Galatians 6:2(NIV)

When we commit to marriage, we commit to numerous things: financial difficulties, family issues, the loss of a job, or health issues. How do we get through all of this? We do that by carrying each other in difficult times, knowing that we will get through whatever we encounter with God on our side. The key to it is to praise God through it all. Be determined to soar above all life tosses at you and do it together. Be faithful to each other, especially when you recognize that it's taking a toll on your mate. Through prayer and companionship, we can lift each other before God. Know that when things look down, feel down, or you feel cast down, He is the lifter of your head. Hold each other up.

Personal Reflection

How does prayer fit in when difficult times come? What does my prayer life look like?

_____

_____

_____

_____

_____

_____

_____

Day 257

Serve wholeheartedly, as if you were serving the Lord, not people.
Ephesians 6:7(NIV)

We should all look to our mates as our kings and queens, and they should be treated with royalty. Whatever we do for each other is done with a smile and attitude, demonstrating our love and affection. The small things we do often show how much we appreciate being married to our spouse. Never let another man or woman compliment your queen or king. Leave for work each day by reassuring them they are that very special part of you! When you do these things, make sure that it comes from the heart. There are many opportunities to demonstrate our love for each other. Be creative in your approach and watch the fringe benefits. Take the time to treat your KING or QUEEN with royalty. If they've stuck with you this far, let's go a little further and show them.

Personal Reflection
What can I do to compliment and support my King/Queen consistently?

_____

_____

_____

_____

_____

_____

Day 258

If I speak in the tongues of men or of angels, but do not have love, I am only a resounding gong or a clanging cymbal. If I have the gift of prophecy and can fathom all mysteries and all knowledge, and if I have a faith that can move mountains, but do not have love, I am nothing. If I give all I possess to the poor and give over my body to hardship that I may boast, but do not have love, I gain nothing.
1 Corinthians 13:1-3(NIV)

Loving your spouse is a learning process. If you've been married a week or a day, your love for each other will be the health of your marriage. By loving them with all you have, you tell them they are a priority in your life. Your actions show this love and is a statement that you have the best interest of your mate before you. Know that this type of love cannot be attained without God. He is the epitome of love in that He loved us so much that He gave us the greatest gift of love. Demonstrate it by showing the love of your life how much you love them, not just by words but also by doing.

Personal Reflection
How can I apply this passage of scripture and nugget to my marriage?

_____

_____

_____

_____

_____

Day 259

Whatever you do, work at it with all your heart, as working for the Lord, not for human masters, 24 since you know that you will receive an inheritance from the Lord as a reward. It is the Lord Christ you are serving.
Colossians 3:23-24(NIV)

Even in marriage, it should be our goal to bring God glory. In our efforts to grow together, first in the knowledge of Him as our Lord and Savior, but to exhibit His attributes in how we show our love to whom God has placed in our life for a marital journey. Our marriage should be an open testimony to those in marriage and those anticipating marriage that it is a growing process. If God is in our plans, come what may, we will survive the worst and best of times. Take every opportunity to work hard at making your marriage work. Never allow outside forces to come against your marriage. Be able to discern when those forces are present, but be swift to pray them away. Everything you do for your spouse and in your marriage, do it as unto the Lord. You do your part, and He will honor His.

Personal Reflection
How can my marriage bring Glory to God? What can I do?

_____

_____

_____

_____

_____

_____

Day 260

Wives, submit yourselves to your husbands, as is fitting in the Lord.
Colossians 3:18(NIV)

Marriage is a partnership, a lasting one at that. It is not an opportunity for the husband to be domineering over his wife or the wife to be controlling. There is mutual respect among the two of you to appreciate what each of you brings to the marriage. We're in this thing together. It will not survive being one-dimensional. Subsequently, it is submitting first to the will of God and then to each other. If you have not submitted to God, it will be quite a task to submit to your spouse. Submission is not being weak but showing humility; what greater lesson can we learn than in how Christ demonstrated the lesson in humility by Him dying for us? Loving each other is just meeting each other's needs. Men love your wives as Christ loved the church. Wives, support and encourage your husband to be the family's spiritual leader. The Word encourages us to rely upon each other. We both have roles to play, but they can only be accomplished with the aid of the Spirit of God.

Husbands, love your wives, just as Christ loved the
church and gave himself up for her.
Ephesians 5:25(NIV)

Personal Reflection

How can we jointly submit to each other and adjust to our differences?

_____

_____

_____

_____

Day 261

Serve wholeheartedly, as if you were serving the Lord, not people.
Ephesians 6:7(NIV)

Marriage involves the connection between two people determined to love each other for the rest of their lives. It's not about what we can get from the marriage but what is gained in the union. When it is ordained and sanctioned by God, it is more than suitable, it's destined to bring Him glory. We honor God by how we treat each other. This is done by living by the Word of God and practicing the principles He has outlined for marriage. Stay faithful to God, your spouse, and watch the benefits that come with your obedience.

Personal Reflection
How can I apply this passage of scripture and nugget to my marriage?

_____

_____

_____

_____

_____

_____

_____

_____

Day 262

Fear thou not; for I am with thee: be not dismayed; for I am thy God:
I will strengthen thee; yea, I will help thee; yea,
I will uphold thee with the right hand of my righteousness.
Isaiah 41:10(KJV)

Mere love will never be enough to sustain a marriage. If it is centered around what you can gain from the connection, not the relationship, it is headed for disaster. No love or marriage can survive without being given to Him from its inception. Only God can keep us through the rough and challenging times, even when we feel that it's about to fold. If He brought us to it, He will take us through it! I thank Him each day for keeping me (individual) in marriage. Had I tried to make it on my own, I know it would have failed long before now. Give your marriage to Him, and let Him be the glue that holds the two of you together. It was His plan from the very beginning.

Personal Reflection
How have I committed myself and my marriage to God?

_____

_____

_____

_____

_____

_____

Day 263

He only is my rock and my salvation: he is my defense; I shall not be moved.
Psalms 62:6(KJV)

Commitment is foundational to your marriage; it's important because you vowed to love each other for the rest of your lives. If we genuinely love each other, that love is reciprocated to each other every passing day. It is your willingness to admit to yourself that you alone cannot love your spouse as you should without the help of God. Love and commitment require you to choose to do it until you feel it becomes a part of your lifestyle. You love each other by showing it and working hard for the relationship. There is a great hymn of the church, and the lyrics state: "On Christ the solid rock I stand, all other ground is sinking sand." Determine that your love for your spouse is rock solid. It is built on a love God has demonstrated to us and transferred to us through our love for one another. Commit to doing whatever is necessary to keep it solid and fruitful. Raise the bar and be in love for the long haul.

Personal Reflection
How can I keep my marriage on the firm foundation of Christ?

_____

_____

_____

_____

_____

_____

Day 264

I will remain in the world no longer, but they are still in the world, and I am coming to you.
Holy Father, protect them by the power of your name, the name you gave me,
so that they may be one as we are one.
John 17:11(NIV)

One of the most critical practices in a marriage is the practice of prayer. During this opportunity, you place your petition before a God who is able and willing to hear your call. Make it a part of your everyday day rituals. Prayer is your vehicle for establishing a lasting relationship with the Creator of marriage. Pray for each other daily, for spiritual covering and the security of your home and children. When you are on good terms with God, you will find that nothing can shake your foundation because He is the one who can hold you and your marriage in the best and worst of times.

Personal Reflection
How can I apply this passage of scripture and nugget to my marriage?

_____

_____

_____

_____

_____

_____

Day 265

But if serving the Lord seems undesirable to you, then choose for yourselves this day whom you will serve, whether the gods your ancestors served beyond the Euphrates, or the gods of the Amorites, in whose land you are living. But as for me and my household, we will serve the Lord.
Joshua 24:15(NIV)

If anything is failing in our society today, it is the institution of the family. We have succumbed to the grab-it-and-get-it mentality of the world, where relationships don't exist, we're just existing. There is a cry for the return of the family, a family that is centered around a love for God and each other. It is mirrored in our lives as we are a part of this world but not of this world. It is a period in time when we must return to a God consciousness that is critical to the structure of the family. Understand that we, the family, are under attack. It is time for leadership in the home to step up. Fathers, as heads of your household and your helpmate, we must make some critical decisions that will affect the atmosphere in our homes. Wives, you must continue to be the nurturer. Our children don't know the way, and they must be taught. Don't compromise. Take a stand as the spiritual head of your home and come against any and everything that seeks to damage your family. Take the stand as Joshua did with his family, "As for me and my house, we will serve the Lord".

Personal Reflection
How can I apply this nugget to build a strong family structure?

_____

_____

_____

_____

Day 266

Your Word is a lamp to my feet and a light to my path.
Psalms 119:105(NKJV)

Whenever we plan a trip, we must map or chart our destiny. It will tell us what routes we will take to lead us to our point of destination. The Word of God is a manual for our life. Everything that we face in this life is outlined in the Bible. The Bible can transform us into what we were purposed to be. The Bible is like a vegetable and should always be a part of our spiritual diet. Biblical principles are critical to the success of your marriage. When was the last time you had an opportunity to discuss the Bible with your spouse or children? Use the Word of God as you make decisions for yourself and your family. If you digest the Word daily, you will be amazed at how much of a difference it will make in your life. The Word of God is the best advice for maintaining a spirit-filled relationship with your spouse and family.

Personal Reflection
How has the Word of God become a part of my marital process?

_____

_____

_____

_____

_____

_____

Day 267

And the two will become one flesh. So, then they are no longer two, but one flesh.
Mark 10:8(NKJV)

Two hearts that beat as one; the essence of a marriage and relationship. No longer are you two individuals, but one. That may sound strange, but when the two of you are committed to being one through the help of God, you will find that it will come easy. Because your relationship with each other is much more than physical or intimate; it is a spiritual and divine institution. Every marriage is a work in progress. Being one can only be attained by being consistent and persistent. It won't happen overnight, but it can and will with a concerted effort between you. Take that step every day and make it happen.

Personal Reflection

How can I help create an atmosphere of oneness in my marriage?

_____

_____

_____

_____

_____

_____

_____

Day 268

That is why a man leaves his father and mother and is united to his wife,
and they become one flesh.
Genesis 2:24(NIV)

Therefore, what God has joined together, let no one separate.
Mark 10:9(NIV)

Marriage was the first instituted and set in place by God. This means that it is important to Him. He saw the need for man to not exist by himself, so he provided for that need by giving him a wife to complete him. In the process, the two would become one and emulate the love God demonstrated to us. His design was that marriage would be a loyal partnership between a man and a woman. It was designed to last; what God has joined together, let no man separate. He purposed it before eternity.

Personal Reflection
How can I apply this passage of scripture and nugget to my marriage?

_____

_____

_____

_____

_____

_____

Day 269

*And he answered and said unto them, have ye not read, that he which made them at the
beginning made them male and female, and said, for this cause shall a man leave father and
mother, and shall cleave to his wife: and they twain shall be one flesh?
Wherefore they are no more twain, but one flesh. What therefore
God hath joined together, let not man put asunder.
Matthew 19:4-6(KJV)*

Oneness was God's original intent from the beginning. He said, "It is not good for man to
be alone." How else would He take woman from man? The woman was made primarily to
complete man. Oneness starts with a friendship that is nurtured and protected. It is God's
purpose for the institution of the family. Your challenge is to commit to whatever is needed
to ensure oneness in your relationship with your spouse. At times, it will require that you
make the necessary sacrifice to meet your spouse's needs. When we become one flesh, there
should never be a need for a husband to think that his wife is his private possession. We
should only apply God's original plan of the flesh of two individuals becoming one.

Personal Reflection

How can I stay on course to follow God's original design for marriage?

_____

_____

_____

_____

_____

_____

Day 270

Be always on the watch, and pray that you may be able to escape all that is about to happen, and that you may be able to stand before the Son of Man.
Luke 21:36 (NIV)

Make sure you do whatever it takes to ensure your marriage is covered spiritually. This means there is always a 24/7 alert to dispel anyone who attempts to come against you and your spouse. How do we do that? We are always prayerful about each other, even when we aren't around each other. Our prayer is that God would protect the one we love from those things that seek to tear our love and relationship apart. In addition to our praying, we are encouraged to watch.

Watch means that we are always alert, on guard, and focused. Marriage and the family are the enemy's targets. His mission is accomplished if he can destroy the marriage and the family. But the DEVIL IS A LIAR! What God has joined together, no man can put asunder or separate. I pray that we will begin to watch, pray, and learn the secrets of having a successful and victorious marriage in Christ Jesus.

Personal Reflection
How have I worked to keep the hand of the enemy out of my marriage?

_____

_____

_____

_____

_____

Day 271

Jesus knew their thoughts and said to them, "Every kingdom divided against itself will be ruined, and every city or household divided against itself will not stand.
Matthew 12:25(NIV)

When we look at the Trinity, we look at the nature of God working in three capacities. Yet, oneness exists, where all operate in the spirit of unity and oneness. In that same spirit, we conduct ourselves as husband and wife, touching and agreeing on the same things.

This is a continuous process in marriage where we always work spiritually and emotionally toward standing together as examples to our children and the many experiences we share. A house divided against itself will not stand and will eventually dissolve. How do we develop this oneness?

How can two people with different wills and bodies survive and live together for the rest of their lives? If we stay true to the original design given by the Creator, that marriage will last until death do us part. Despite the ups and downs we experience, there is a work in progress to remain faithful to the commitment made to God and each other. Through the power of prayer and the guidance of the Holy Spirit, it can be done. As we work on loving each other unconditionally and striving to make our marriages work, we will surely experience the wondrous working power of God as we move toward oneness.

Personal Reflection
How can I help keep the unity of my family and my marriage a priority?

_____

_____

_____

_____

_____

_____

_____

_____

_____

Personal Reflection
How can I apply this passage of scripture and nugget to my marriage?

_____

_____

_____

_____

_____

_____

_____

_____

Day 272

Love must be sincere. Hate what is evil, cling to what is good.
Be devoted to one another in love. Honor one another above yourselves.
Romans 12:9-10 (NIV)

The person you've been married to is someone that you feel connected to. There is no limit to what you will do to meet every emotional, spiritual, and physical need. Your needs are never placed before theirs, and your desire should be to learn their love language. Always provide an atmosphere that is filled with love and respect for each other. Validate your love for each other every time the opportunity presents itself. There can never be a limit to the number of times we say to each other, I Love You.

Personal Reflection
How am I meeting the needs of the one I love?

_____

_____

_____

_____

_____

_____

Day 273

Two are better than one, because they have good return for their labor:
If either falls down, one can help the other up.
Ecclesiastes 4:9-10(NIV)

This year marks the 43rd year of marriage to my best friend and my lover for life. She has been my biggest fan from day one. It has not always been rosy, but through prayer and the grace of God, we are still standing and standing STRONG. We are now in the best years of our lives where we enjoy each other, laughing, spending quality time together, having pleasant conversations, and remaining in love. I thank God for her because we have learned to appreciate what each other brings to the marriage. We now have our best day before us, and I look forward to what God has in store for us in the coming days. I'm thankful to God that my spouse was God-sent.

It has been easy loving my spouse over the years. And yes, we had some rough times, but we stood through them together with the help of God. I tell my spouse that when God designed her for me, He gave me absolutely the BEST. There is no doubt that she is my rib. She has been a true love in my life. Thank you for being the loving spouse you have been and bringing out the best in me. There is none other like you.

With that being said, learn to appreciate one another and always look for the best in each other. We pray that God will bless every marriage to live a life of true love and commitment to one another. Keep God's covering over your marriage through prayer.

Personal Reflection
How have I learned to appreciate the love of my life?

_____

_____

_____

_____

_____

_____

Personal Reflection
How can I apply this passage of scripture and nugget to my marriage?

_____

_____

_____

_____

_____

_____

_____

_____

Day 274

Therefore, if you have any encouragement from being united with Christ, if any comfort from his love, if any common sharing in the spirit, if any tenderness and compassion, then make my joy complete by being like-minded, have the same love, being one in spirit and of one mind. Do nothing out of selfish ambition or vain conceit. Rather in humility value others above yourselves, not looking to your own interests but each of you to the interest of the others.
Philippians 2:1-4(NIV)

The Bible says a man should leave his father and mother and cleave to his wife. Cleaving involves a sense of connecting, the act of unifying. Unity in marriage is so important to your relationship. This means a total commitment to each other. When things get tough, it is not a time to run back home or to others; it is a time of coming together and making things work for the good of your relationship and your marriage, seeking to improve it. Cleaving is one of God's elements for marriage. Work hard at it, and watch your unity and closeness develop.

Personal Reflection
What can I do to better connect with my spouse?

_____

_____

_____

_____

_____

_____

Day 275

The steps of a good man are ordered by the Lord: and he delighteth in his way.
Psalms 37:23(KJV)

The Word of God gives us a spiritual principle we can use even in the process of growing together in oneness. If any two of you shall agree on earth as touching anything they ask, it shall be done for them of my Father, who is in heaven. (Matthew 18:19KJV) As a couple, if we are on one accord with God, He will give us the direction we need in any situation. It may be a career move that may affect the other, an investment that may affect the entire family; in all that we do, we must ensure that our directives are from the one who made us and purposed our union together. If we are aligned with His will, we will find ourselves in the safety of the Lord. In ALL our ways, we must acknowledge God, and HE WILL direct our paths, even when they don't seem apparent to us.

Personal Reflection
How are we including God in our marital goals and dreams?

_____

_____

_____

_____

_____

_____

Day 276

Anyone who does not provide for their relatives, and especially for their own household, has denied the faith and is worse than an unbeliever.
1 Timothy 5:8(NIV)

Cleaving is a relational word that has the connotations of bonding or gluing. This is meaningful for a marriage because it expresses the commitment and consecration of a husband and a wife to each other. God's purpose and plan for marriage is that spouses belong to each other in the physical relationship. One of the leading causes of marriages breaking up is the lack of oneness in all aspects of their marriage. The marriage suffers because one or both spouses are more committed to themselves than to each other. Your marriage is the most important thing in your life except for your relationship with God. Nothing, I mean NOTHING, should take priority over your marriage and your family. For those of us in ministry, don't get so ministry-minded that you forget your mate and your family. Remember that the family was created before the church. How would you rate your cleaving?

Personal Reflection
How can I apply this passage of scripture and nugget to my marriage?

_____

_____

_____

_____

_____

Day 277

With Christ, ALL things are possible.
If a house is divided against itself, that house cannot stand.
Mark 3:25(NIV)

There is something remarkable about being in unity with one another, especially when that someone is the one you love. Unity is about oneness. In our marriages, we have to find love and passion for each other, even in the midst of our differences. Will we ever agree on everything? No, but we will strive to work toward that oneness so that we can still agree to disagree and it does not affect our differences or our oneness.

We demonstrate oneness when we have a team mentality, knowing that it is never about us individually but collectively. You will find that without the two of you being unified, your relationships will unravel and operate in disarray. I would impress upon those with children to always keep your children from seeing you divided. Settle all differences in private. It is not an overnight thing; it is ongoing!! Remember, a house divided against itself CANNOT stand.

Personal Reflection
How can I stay on course to follow God's original design for marriage?

_____

_____

_____

_____

_____

Day 278

For this reason, a man shall leave his father and mother and be united to his wife,
and the two will become one flesh.
Ephesians 5:31(NIV)

Therefore, shall a man leave his father and mother and cleave unto his wife: and they shall be one flesh. God has ordained this process since the beginning of creation. Cleaving involves a connection to another without involvement from anyone else. When two people are joined, they are bound to commit to each other despite difficulties and individual differences. It means discussing things and seeking God's wisdom in every situation we experience during our marriage.

Cleaving was God's original intent for a couple that aspire to be joined in holy matrimony. It is a serious matter that shouldn't be taken lightly. In the sight of our Creator you become one in the flesh, flowing together to serve Him. Remember that God holds us responsible for doing all we can to maintain that bond between us.

Personal Reflection
How can I apply this passage of scripture and nugget to my marriage?

_____

_____

_____

_____

_____

Day 279

That all of them may be one, Father, just as you are in me and I am in you. May they also be in us so that the world may believe that you have sent me.
John 17:21(NIV)

In marriage, there should always be a sense of teamwork, always striving to speak with one voice despite differences, which will always lead to significant conflicts. It should be our goal as partners in marriage to first strive for a spiritual union with God. When God is placed at the center of our marriage, we can rest assured that we can face whatever difficulties are presented to us. Our marriage together is one of the greatest blessings to a husband and a wife. We learn through the Word that unity was important to God because He knew it was not good for man to be alone, so He created woman. Through this union and connection, we fulfill the need for oneness and companionship.

I am the vine; you are the branches. If you remain in me and I in you, you will bear much fruit; apart from me you can do nothing.
John 15:5(NIV)

Personal Reflection
How can I apply this passage of scripture and nugget to my marriage?

_____

_____

_____

_____

_____

Day 280

*The husband should fulfill his marital duty to his wife,
and likewise, the wife to her husband.*
1 Corinthians 7:3(NIV)

Those of us who are committed to each other are called to respect each other's God-given roles in marriage. That is to be committed to each other till death. The Bible says that man should love his wife like Christ loves the church. He has assigned us different roles, but all we do in our marriage is to bring honor to God. We were designed from the beginning to complement each other.

Our role as husbands is to put our wife's well-being and comfort before our own. This is reciprocated by the wife. The husband and the wife must submit to each other. It is a never-ending process of sharing the same goals and honoring the vows between you. Commitment is never a one-way street, but it's God's way of bringing us to oneness.

Personal Reflection
How can sharing and submitting to each other create a lasting commitment?

_____

_____

_____

_____

_____

Day 281

Except the Lord build the house, they labour in vain that build it:
except the Lord keep the city, the watchman waketh but in vain.
Psalms 127:1(KJV)

I'm sure we can remember how exciting it was when we first met our spouses, how we romanced and burned with passion. It continued, even to the day of your wedding vows, but then something happened to smother the flames. Somewhere during the course of things, we lost the zeal for marriage, and it became stale. Marriage is more than just cohabitating and living in the same house.

It's like a winter fire; you never let it go out. You add a log here, and you add a log there to keep the fire burning. Our marriage, relationship, and our romance are like building a house. The structure of our home is contingent upon what we make it with and what we build it on. If we build on sand or a shaky foundation, it will be vulnerable to the plethora of attacks the enemy throws at us. If it is built on the principles of God, a firm foundation, nothing and no one can shake what you have as a couple. Every day is spent enjoying the company of your spouse. There will be some windy days and rough seas, but because it's built on a rock, it WILL stand! God loves when His PLAN comes together!!

Personal Reflection
What am I doing to keep my marriage alive and vibrant?

_____

_____

_____

_____

Day 282

The Lord God said, "It is not good for the man to be alone.
I will make a helper suitable for him.
Genesis 2:18(NIV)

While the man had everything at his disposal in the garden, there was still a missing ingredient. So, God, in His infinite wisdom, created a help mate. Why? Because she, the woman, completed him. God's original intent for a man and woman was that their connection would be inseparable. Through nurturing our marriage and relationship, we reflect the essence of who God is.

God intended for us to depend upon each other, a support system where the two become one. Those of us who are married are blessed to be part of a unique process. This includes our relationship with our Creator and a covenant relationship with our partners for life. Therefore, tell your spouse daily that they are more than enough for you, because they complete you.

Personal Reflection
How can I apply this passage of scripture and nugget to my marriage?

_____

_____

_____

_____

_____

Day 283

Marriage should be honored by all, and the marriage bed kept pure,
for God will judge the adulterer and all the sexually immoral.
Hebrews 13:4(NIV)

The Word does say that marriage is honorable (Hebrews 13:4 NKJV). The first clause of verse 4 is a declaration of the purpose and design of marriage. That means our commitment is to one woman and one woman only, as well as only one man. Anything outside the bounds of matrimony is unacceptable. It is a bond that can only be separated by death. Every effort is made during our relationship and marriage to satisfy the needs of our spouse. There should be no room for love to be received outside of your marriage.

This passage does not only speak to the sexual part of your marriage, but it speaks to the whole marriage. It's your love language, edifying your spouse, showing care and respect. When we are consumed with the happiness of our spouse and meeting their every need, there is never room to be wooed by another. It'll take ALL your energy to take care of that ONE person!!

Personal Reflection
What is my spouse's love language? How am I fulfilling it?

_____

_____

_____

_____

_____

Day 284

The wife does not have authority over her own body but yields it to her husband.
In the same way, the husband does not have authority
over his own body but yields it to his wife.
1 Corinthians 7:4(NIV)

There should never be a time to withhold ourselves from our spouse. That's why it is so important to resolve all of your issues with each other so that they don't interfere with your lovemaking and time of affection. Also, it may mean agreeing to disagree and moving on. There's nothing worse than loving your spouse, and it is not reciprocated. It leaves your relationship open to outside forces, fulfilling what you should do as a wife or husband.

There will be times in our marriage when our schedules will be busy with work, children, or other priorities. Couples must make concessions to provide quality time with each other. Being tired and busy should never be an excuse to spend that intimate time with each other. Make every effort to capture those special times together with your lover for life.

Personal Reflection
How am I working to resolve conflict? How are we making time for each other?

_____

_____

_____

_____

_____

Day 285

Do not have sexual relations with your neighbor's
wife and defile yourself with her.
Leviticus 18:20(NIV)

Our spouses should be the only one who provides for our sexual needs. This will help to sway either of us from seeking those desires from someone else. Make sure that those needs are met. We are responsible for the sexual behaviors of each other. If our desires go south, it may be due to our being so involved in other things that we forget to fulfill the needs of our spouse. If there is a void to be filled, YOU are to be the one to fill it. Make sure there is never room for the enemy to try and put thoughts in your spouse's mind regarding their needs and who should fulfill them.

Personal Reflection
How can I apply this passage of scripture and nugget to my marriage?

_____

_____

_____

_____

_____

_____

_____

Day 286

Husbands, love your wives, even as Christ also loved the church, and gave
Himself for it. So, ought men to love their wives as their own bodies.
He that loveth his wife loveth himself.
Ephesians 5:25-28(KJV)

In marriage, there is always an act of giving, giving your best to meet the needs and desires of your lover. It's never about selfish motives but about what I can do to ensure that my mate is physically, mentally, and spiritually satisfied. Giving this type of love is continuous and unending. It is selfishness that lends itself to working with the enemy to break down the walls of marriage and cause us to ponder the idea of separation and divorce.

If we look at marriage, we can see it as Paul speaks about Christ's relationship with the church. He tells us to love each other as Christ loves the church, who gave of Himself as a sacrifice for the sake of love. If we love with this kind of love, we will conform to God's original design for marriage at the beginning of creation.

Personal Reflection
What am I doing to ensure the sustainability of our marriage?

_____

_____

_____

_____

_____

Day 287

Greater love has no one than this, than to lay down one's life for his friends.
John 15:13(NKJV)

Having the love of Christ is a unique phenomenon. If we look at the love of Christ, He loves us with whatever we bring to the table. Whatever flaws and shortcomings, they are all seen in a spirit of love. I often wonder how God could love someone so messed up as we are. Regardless of how messed up we are, He will receive us again.

If we have the love of Christ, we will do what is necessary, never to cause displeasure to the one we love. When we think of doing anything that would hurt our mate, we should be reminded of our love for each other. Think about the word friend. True friends are always concerned about the welfare of their friends. Friends will never intentionally try to hurt their friends. Because our spouse is our friend, our ultimate goal is the satisfaction of the one we love.

Personal Reflection
How can I apply this passage of scripture and nugget to my marriage?

_____

_____

_____

_____

_____

_____

Day 288

You were bought at a price. Therefore, honor God with your bodies.
1 Corinthians 6:20(NIV)

Intimacy is the closeness and connection that is established between a man and a woman. It's making a statement that every day is another day I will bring joy to my lover. What will happen if we neglect to do so and you are denied the chance to do so by some circumstances? Every day is a chance to show that love to your spouse. Never take it for granted. Take the time to show it by every means necessary. That means making the time to share your intimate moments.

Personal Reflection
How can I apply this passage of scripture and nugget to my marriage?

_____

_____

_____

_____

_____

_____

_____

Day 289

How beautiful you are and how pleasing, my love, with your delights.
Song of Solomon 7:6(NIV)

When did you last compliment or say something nice to your spouse? It's not just something we say during the courtship but maintained throughout our marriage. What is more important is that the compliments come from you, not an outsider. If we don't validate our love for each other at home, someone is waiting to do what you won't do. Don't leave a crack in your relationship for that. Find your mate, or call them now to tell them something special. They will be glad you've not lost that loving feeling.

Personal Reflection

What do we do to compliment and validate each other?

_____

_____

_____

_____

_____

_____

_____

Day 290

Also, if two lie down together, they will keep warm.
But how can one keep warm alone?
Ecclesiastes 4:11(NIV)

From the beginning, God said it was not good for man to be alone. In His creative divine thinking, He created someone to complete a man. Those of us who have been allowed to be blessed with a spouse can enjoy the completeness of having that person to confide in, share your life with, and spend times of intimacy together. Consider your marriage a high-maintenance relationship because it is a constant work in progress to maintain a healthy and intimate relationship. Intimacy is more than being physical, it's sharing your heart and thoughts with your spouse. This process develops a deeper understanding of your love and commitment to each other.

Personal Reflection
How can I apply this passage of scripture and nugget to my marriage?

_____

_____

_____

_____

_____

_____

Day 291

Love is patient, love is kind. It does not envy, it does not boast,
it is not proud. It does not dishonor others, it is not self-seeking,
it is not easily angered, it keeps not record of wrongs.
1 Corinthians 13:4-5(NIV)

Marriage is a union between two individuals. Never should it be a one-way street. The joy of marriage is the meshing of two hearts that compliment each other. All of our efforts are spent to bring happiness to each other. Love is not selfish, but it is putting the best interest of your mate as your priority. When we function together, we flow in the same direction. Whatever load is carried, both are responsible for sharing in carrying the load. There is no other answer to a successful relationship or marriage. In marriage, one plus one equals ONE.

Personal Reflection
How can I apply this passage of scripture and nugget to my marriage?

_____

_____

_____

_____

_____

_____

Day 292

Now eagerly desire the greater gifts. And yet I will show you the most excellent way.
1 Corinthians 12:31(NIV)

In the process of becoming one, there is a meshing of personalities, attitudes, and differences that somehow compliment each other. There may be a lack in a mate that may be compensated by the other mate that helps to bring the other best in your relationship. Remember, a woman was created at creation because she helped to fill a void that existed, so man became complete when she was created. It's not about one of you taking a dominant role in your marriage but that you enhance each other. We should bring out the best in each other. Two hearts that beat as one.

And the Lord said, "It is not good that man should be alone;
I will make him a helper comparable to him.
Genesis 2:18(NKJV)

Personal Reflection
How do I work to fulfill my role as a soul mate and lover for life?

_____

_____

_____

_____

_____

Day 293

*He who dwells in the secret place of the Most High
shall abide under the shadow of the Almighty.
I will say of the Lord, "He is my refuge and my fortress;
My God, in Him will I trust."
Psalms 91:1-2(NKJV)*

When the two of you walk hand in hand in love and marriage, your thoughts, hopes, and dreams are merged to form a lasting commitment to each other. Walking together is a true testament that love can and will last. By walking together, we build on the elements crucial to survival through communication, listening, prayer, and a strong belief system. When God is in the process, there is nothing that can tear your marriage and relationship apart.

Personal Reflection
How can I apply this passage of scripture and nugget to my marriage?

_____

_____

_____

_____

_____

_____

Day 294

But pity anyone who falls and has no one to help them up.
Ecclesiastes 4:9-10(NIV)

Our marriages require a lot of attention from both of us. As we strive to make our marriages work, it is clear that we need each other more than ever. There is never a time that we are not co-laborers in a God-ordained union. Nothing is ever done with selfish intent but within a spirit of unity and oneness. We live, and we breathe for each other. The more we support each other, the stronger our love grows and the deeper our commitment. Two are better than one, because they have a good return for their labor. If either of them falls down, one can help the other up.

Personal Reflection

How can I apply this passage of scripture and nugget to my marriage?

_____

_____

_____

_____

_____

_____

Day 295

But seek ye first the kingdom of God,
and his righteousness; and all these things shall be added unto you.
Matthew 6:33(NKJV)

God had a unique and divine thought in the creation process when He created differences, no one with the same DNA, fingerprints, or way of thinking. We are all unique in our own way. We bring to the marriage a plethora of differences that can complete and compliment our relationships. Being spiritual partners, we recognize that we come to build our relationships and merge our lives to create what God has designed our marriage to be. This is a sacred partnership where we accept each other's differences, which will result in a solid and happy marriage.

Personal Reflection
How can I better appreciate the differences we bring to our marriage?

_____

_____

_____

_____

_____

_____

Day 296

Therefore encourage one another and build each other up,
just as in fact you are doing.
1 Thessalonians 5:11(NIV)

A woman has power, and God has given her the privilege and ability to bring life to her husband and their family. A woman invests her time and energies into helping to make him what God has designed. The investments of the woman bring the needed dividends to her relationship with her husband. She sees things in him that he may never see in himself. On the flip side, she also has the power to tear down if misused.

The more a wife affirms her husband, the more she is helping to build what God has planned for his life, which includes YOU. Knowing this, ladies, how are you using the power God has given you to benefit your husband and your marriage? Likewise, my brothers, we have the awesome responsibility to edify those we love and speak life to the one we chose to be our lover for life.

Personal Reflection
How am I consistently seeking to affirm my spouse as I should?

_____

_____

_____

_____

_____

Day 297

No weapon formed against you shall prosper,
and every tongue which rises against you in judgment you
shall condemn. This is the heritage of the servants of the Lord,
and their righteousness is from Me, says the Lord.
Isaiah 54:17(NKJV)

In becoming one flesh, we strive to understand and respect each other's individuality. It will always be a process, but we should never deny each other's right to be an individual first. Though we may differ in our perspective, it should never lead to confrontation. The both of you can remain yourselves as you strive for unity. Many times, you will find that your differences will compliment each other. There's a phrase in an old familiar song relative to our individual differences that speaks to all of us as we strive to achieve oneness: "I love you just the way you are."

Personal Reflection
How can I apply this passage of scripture and nugget to my marriage?

_____

_____

_____

_____

_____

_____

Day 298

Trust in the Lord with all your heart, and lean not on your own understanding;
In all your ways acknowledge Him, and He shall direct your paths.
Proverbs 3:5-6(NKJV)

There is nothing like being unified in marriage. When you realize that we are like the parts of the body, you will see that you can't function without each other. In making decisions, buying a new house, making decisions for our families, we're in this thing together. If we both trust God, we will find that we are more vital than ever because we stand together. Weapons will form to break and separate you, but we have that blessed assurance that nothing and nobody can separate what God has joined together. Every day you have together is a blessing. Stay connected!!

Personal Reflection
How can I apply this passage of scripture and nugget to my marriage?

_____

_____

_____

_____

_____

_____

Day 299

And over all these virtues put on love, which binds them all together in perfect unity.
Colossians 3:14(NIV)

Love and marriage go hand in hand: a mutual affection and commitment to each other. When we love each other, our motives should always be about what is important to us as husband and wife. Our love, among other things, will be the glue that holds us together and keeps us united. It will keep us in all kinds of weather, but it can't be done without the help of God. Jesus has said that a man should love his wife as Christ loves the church. Therefore, your love expressed for each other is equivalent to the same value He has placed on the church.

Personal Reflection
How can I apply this passage of scripture and nugget to my marriage?

_____

_____

_____

_____

_____

_____

_____

Day 300

Love does not delight in evil but rejoices with the truth.
1 Corinthians 13:6 (NIV)

Trust is an ongoing process; it starts long before you exchange vows with each other. Trust is taking each other at your word and having faith in each other. It entails fully communicating with each other, always sharing, and being honest. Marriages will not last without trust and most likely end in separation or divorce. When you have invested your time and energy in building trust in your marriage, you will always feel secure with your spouse. It is that trust that will hold you both together. But remember, once it is broken, rebuilding will take time and work. Let trust be one of the building blocks in the foundation on which your relationship is built.

Personal Reflection
How is trust demonstrated in my marriage?

_____

_____

_____

_____

_____

_____

_____

Day 301

Trust in the Lord with all thine heart; and lean not unto thine own understanding.
In all thy ways acknowledge Him, and He shall direct thy paths.
Proverbs 3:5-6 (KJV)

There is one thing we should keep in mind as we look at the survival of our marriage. God should be the center and foundation of your relationship with your spouse. If He is placed at the center, everything about your marriage will revolve around Him and the principles He has ordained for the marriage. We must utilize the sources and resources He provides for us as His children. If He has ordained it, it can never be compromised, and nothing that comes against it will cause your love for each other to shift. Remember that you are part of a God ordained union, the institution of marriage. Pray each day that the depth of love for each other is increased and that He will give you what is needed to make your marriage last, come hell or high waters. When He is included in our plans, He will honor His promise that nothing can separate us. That's enough for us to rejoice in.

Personal Reflection
How do I keep Christ at the center of my life and marriage?

_____

_____

_____

_____

_____

_____

Day 302

Now be pleased to bless the house of your servant, that it may continue forever in your sight; for you, Sovereign LORD, have spoken, and with your blessing the house of your servant will be blessed forever."
2 Samuel 7:29 (NIV)

A husband and wife make a powerful declaration when they say, God, we dedicate our family and all we have to you. We give God full ownership of our marriage, family, children, and possessions and ask Him to use us for His honor. When God is in the equation of a marriage, there is nothing that you can't get through. He has given the husband the task of being the spiritual leader of his home, the protector, provider, priest, and prophet. A God-fearing husband and wife will recognize the severity of their responsibilities and surrender themselves to the will and authority of God. It is our job to step up and be an influential light to our families and future generations.

Personal Reflection
How am I covering my marriage and family in prayer?

_____

_____

_____

_____

_____

_____

Day 303

In everything give thanks; for this is the will of God in Christ Jesus concerning you.
1 Thessalonians 5:18 (KJV)

As we embrace this new day of thanksgiving, we pray that you are grateful for where God has brought you in your marriages. Though we have witnessed some rough and exciting days, we have remained faithful to the task of being committed to our vows. We can look at each other and see evidence of God's handiwork. We've become better husbands and wives because our commitment to each other and our families remains a priority, a realization that we can do nothing without God. We hope you took the time and thanked God for where you are today and where He is taking your marriage. Though it has not always been rosy, we are grateful that every bump in the road has led us back to Him. It is through Him that we are given what we need to sustain us and our marriage. Lord, we give you praise and thanksgiving for all this and more.

Personal Reflection
How do I give thanks to God for his goodness and my family?

_____

_____

_____

_____

_____

_____

Day 304

And whatsoever ye do, do it heartily, as to the Lord, and not unto men;
Knowing that of the Lord ye shall receive the reward of the inheritance:
for ye serve the Lord Christ.
Colossians 3:23-24(KJV)

When we celebrate the success of our spouse, we are on our way to establishing a bond and a support system for each other. It is also wise to celebrate your marriage's small successes because it helps boost your happiness together as your joys and accomplishments are shared. As you celebrate, it brings glory to God, and your marriage becomes a model to others. It can also be a living demonstration to your children as you celebrate the successes of each other. Be attentive to each other as you look for those things in your lives together to celebrate. To God be the Glory.

Personal Reflection
How can I strive to bring glory to God through my marriage?

_____

_____

_____

_____

_____

_____

Day 305

I will be careful to lead a blameless life when will you come to me?
I will conduct the affairs of my house with a blameless heart.
Psalms 101:2(NIV)

A strong and thriving marriage is built upon a level of trust and being honest with each other. Your actions demonstrate your integrity by what you say and what you do. Brothers, it may be small to us, but our word means a lot to our wives. If we say we will do something, they are looking for us to act upon it. Honor your word by doing your best to fulfill whatever you have promised. The trust we should have for each other is built upon the love we demonstrate daily. Can you be trusted? How good is your word to your spouse?

Personal Reflection
How can I apply this passage of scripture and nugget to my marriage?

_____

_____

_____

_____

_____

_____

Day 306

Unless the Lord builds the house, they labor in vain who build it;
Unless the Lord guards the city, The watchman stays awake in vain.
Psalms 127:1 (NKJV)

One of the great benefits of marriage is the realization that your strength lies in the hands of the Creator, God. If our marriage is rooted and grounded in Him, nothing can shake or break us. Our faith in God is like the root system of the palm tree wrapped around a rock. Christ is the rock that we stand on. We may bend but never break because He is the joy and strength of our lives.

Personal Reflection
How can I apply this passage of scripture to strengthen my marriage?

_____

_____

_____

_____

_____

_____

_____

Day 307

Again, I say to you, that if two of you shall agree on earth as touching anything that they shall ask, it shall be done for them of my Father which is in heaven.
Matthew 18:19(KJV)

Teamwork is so crucial to a marriage. It involves the two of you walking together hand in hand with everything that concerns you, your family, and your marriage. When we are married we are connected to someone else in a way that everything you do is affected by it. God's plan and purpose is that we encourage each other and become that support system that will sustain us in difficult times. When we work against each other we cause discord which can spill over to your entire family. We need each other in a loving way as we strive to be like-minded and having the "oneness" that is so necessary for our survival. Together you can conquer anything; with God in the formula.

Personal Reflection
How can I work in my marriage to create a spirit of teamwork?

_____

_____

_____

_____

_____

_____

Day 308

Where there is no counsel, the people fall;
But in the multitude of counselors there is safety.
Proverbs 11:14 (NKJV)

It is always good to have good relationships with couples who have endured the ups and downs of marriage. As you strive in your marriage to become one, it is good to seek the counsel of godly couples, ones that you respect and value their advice. They may be people you have observed who could give you sound advice in parenting, being a godly wife and husband, or during critical decisions. The counsel they will provide should be godly and not what they think or feel, that's an intrusion. That's why you should seek the wisdom of those who have proven themselves over the years to be true to the sanctity of marriage. Take the time and seek God for direction in your marriage.

The decisions that you make for your marriage and your family will ultimately be yours. Be a discerner of the advice you are given; know that it is God-given. It is a blessing to have those in your church community who can share how God has worked in their marriage through the years. Listen and grab hold of the marital nuggets to gain from their wisdom.

Personal Reflection
How do I seek godly counsel and wisdom in my marriage?

_____

_____

_____

_____

Day 309

The way of fools seems right to them, but the wise listen to advice.
Proverbs 12:15(NIV)

Solomon, one of the wisest men in biblical history, tells us to listen to advice that can be shared with others. If we want our marriages to survive, our first step is acknowledging God in all our doings. One way to avoid challenges in your marriage is first to be committed to it; in times of problems or trouble, seek the wisdom of godly people. Wisdom is important in all situations. The Word of God tells us if we lack wisdom, we should always seek God. When seeking the wisdom and advice of others, be sure that they are people of God who believe that marriage is honorable in His sight.

Personal Reflection
How can I apply this passage of scripture and nugget to my marriage?

_____

_____

_____

_____

_____

_____

_____

Day 310

I am the vine; you are the branches. If you remain in me and I in you,
you will bear much fruit; apart from me you can do nothing.
Matthew 15:5 (NKJV)

The key to survival in a marriage is that God is at the center of all you do. He has to be the one whom you consult through prayers. When the two of you acknowledge that you know nothing about anything, then you are in the right position for Him to guide and direct you. The Word says that the beginning of wisdom comes when you reverence God. He is the designer and orchestrator of marriage; who else can lead you but the One who sanctioned it? It is in Him that you are directed and protected through every storm, every test, and every trial. He can better bless us when we abide under the auspices of His divine wisdom. He is our power source!!

Personal Reflection
How do I acknowledge God as the source of my being and marriage?

_____

_____

_____

_____

_____

_____

Day 311

A person finds joy in giving an apt reply, and how good is a timely word!
Proverbs 15:23 (NIV)

Nothing is better than having those around you who are seasoned in their marriages. They serve as great models for what marriage is all about. Many of us had to learn on the fly, but we were fortunate to have those couples who saw something in us as a couple. They were always there to give us sound advice while not being intrusive. Much is to be gained by taking on godly married mentors who can bless you and your marriage.

Personal Reflection
How can I apply this passage of scripture to my marriage?

_____

_____

_____

_____

_____

_____

_____

Day 312

But encourage one another daily, as long as it is called,
"Today, so that none of you may be hardened by sin's deceitfulness."
Hebrews 3:13(NIV)

Taking the time each day to say something to encourage your spouse will strengthen your marriage. When the both of you become your #1 fan, you will find that there will be nothing and no one that can come between what the two of you have together. There is power in encouraging each other; it helps to bring out the best in you. This can only happen when husbands see their wives as their queens and wives see their husbands as kings. We are good for each other when we can see the best in each other. Create an atmosphere of love and encouragement, and see your relationship flourish. Blessings upon you and your marriage.

Personal Reflection
What am I doing in my marriage to encourage and support my spouse?

_____

_____

_____

_____

_____

_____

_____

Day 313

So then, each of us will give an account of ourselves to God.
Romans 14:12(NIV)

As we are accountable to each other as husband and wife, so are we ultimately accountable to our God. REMEMBER, we promised to love, honor, and keep each other, even when we don't feel it. One way to be accountable to each other is by performing our responsibilities as husband and wife. When we honor those promises, what will follow will be the blessings of God. Be the husband and wife that God calls you and expects you to be.

Personal Reflection

How are we holding each other accountable in our marital commitment?

_____

_____

_____

_____

_____

_____

_____

Day 314

For lack of guidance a nation falls, but victory is won through many advisers.
Proverbs 11:14(NIV)

The Word says that a fool's way seems right in his own eyes, but a wise man listens for advice. Throughout your marriage, you will get advice from many people who are close to you. Most important is that you can discern the merit of the advice. You make sure that what was given was scriptural and godly. Never receive advice when they are telling you what to do. When it all boils down, pray to the Lord for direction. He has proven throughout history that He will never fail you. He will be faithful to His Word.

Personal Reflection

How am I seeking God for his wisdom in my life and marriage?

_____

_____

_____

_____

_____

_____

_____

_____

Day 315

Plans fail for lack of counsel, but with many advisers they succeed.
Proverbs 15:22(NIV)

If you want to send your marriage in the direction of failure, seek ungodly advice. There will be periods in your marriage when you may want to pursue other perspectives from your friends and family, but I caution you to be cautious of what you receive. All of us are genuinely unqualified to advise as we, too, are looking for wisdom in our marriages as well. Still, God allows our marriages to serve as a testimony to others regarding how He can bring us through any dark situation. Know that the wisdom you need in challenging moments comes from God Himself. He should be your first source as you pray and meditate on trying times in your marriage. The advice given by others may not always fit your marriage. Stand on the premise that "true" wisdom only comes from our Creator. Seek Him in all you do.

Personal Reflection
How can I apply this passage of scripture and nugget to my marriage?

_____

_____

_____

_____

_____

_____

Day 316

Your word is a lamp for my feet, a light on my path.
Psalm 119:105(NIV)

Having the Word of God as a part of your marriage is vital. The Word can bring so much energy to your marriage and support any problem you may experience. When time is spent in the Word, you will find that you can better cope with whatever comes your way; it's like being on a good diet, and you feel better because of it. When you are FULL of the Word, you can speak to situations. Spend time in the Word, and when times of difficulty come, let the Word do the work!!

Personal Reflection
How much time am I spending in the Word for my spiritual and personal growth?

_____

_____

_____

_____

_____

_____

_____

Day 317

These are the things God has revealed to us by His Spirit.
The Spirit searches all things, even the deep things of God.
1 Corinthians 2:10(NIV)

The Word of God is our road map to whatever we experience. Dig deep into God's Word and discover all of the promises He has for you and yours. The promises of God are yes and amen. Do you know what He has promised those who love Him? His Word gives life and can bring joy to your marriage; make it a part of your day.

Personal Reflection

How is God orchestrating the course of my marriage and my life?

_____

_____

_____

_____

_____

_____

_____

Day 318

I seek you with all my heart; do not let me stray from your commands.
I have hidden your word in my heart that I might not sin against you.
Psalms 119:10-11(NIV)

The Bible is filled with the promises of God. To know what they are, you must first read His Word. What's so good about His promises? Every promise that He has made, you can depend on. It is the Word that will build your relationship with God as well as your relationship with each other. Let it be a part of your everyday spiritual diet; then, you can rely on every promise He has made.

Personal Reflection
How can I apply this passage of scripture and nugget to my marriage?

_____

_____

_____

_____

_____

_____

_____

Day 319

Let the word of Christ dwell in you richly in all wisdom, teaching and admonishing one another in psalms and hymns and spiritual songs, Singing with grace in your hearts to the Lord.
Colossians 3:16(NKJV)

2 Timothy 2:15 tells us that we should diligently study the Word of God. It helps deepen our understanding of who God is and His will for our lives. The Word of God is more valuable than anything this life offers. It is our GPS to steer us in the ways of God. The Psalmist in Psalms 119:105 tells us how beneficial His Word is to us; Thy Word is a lamp unto my feet and a light unto my path.

Personal Reflection
How much time am I delegating to study the Word of God?

_____

_____

_____

_____

_____

_____

Day 320

Not forsaking the assembling of ourselves together, as the manner of some is, but exhorting one another, and so much the more, as you see the day approaching.
Hebrews 10:25 (KJV)

The Bible can be deep and challenging. That's why being part of a church where the Word is faithfully taught and preached is so important. Hearing it explained in sermons and Bible study classes gives you a broader, more balanced view of what God is saying through His Word. You'll also get to join others on the same journey you are. It is good that the church is a part of your marriage; in it lies a connection to those who are also of the household of faith. You and your family will be interwoven with other families as the testimonies of others will bless you. As the wife is the bride of the husband, so is the church the bride of Christ. Upon His return, He will come to receive His bride. There can be no greater joy in your lives as husband and wife than to be connected to the Creator. If your marriage is not operating under a covering, find a Bible-driven church and watch God move in your lives.

Personal Reflection
How am I assuring myself, my spouse, and my family's connection to God?

_____

_____

_____

_____

_____

_____

Day 321

Unless the Lord builds the house, they labor in vain that build it.
Psalms 127:1(NKJV)

It is important to make your marriage a top priority that is built upon every moment you spend with your spouse. There must be a time when we connect emotionally, spiritually, and physically. That foundation must be laid initially and worked on during your lives together. If built effectively, it will be that solid base that would be necessary when the struggles and challenges of marriage present themselves. Commit to putting the time and effort into creating a oneness driven by respect, trust, and nurturing. Remember that your first foundation is your relationship with the Creator. When life issues come upon you, there will be nothing you can't survive. He'll be the source and sustainer on your journey of marriage as long as you remain rooted and grounded in Him.

Personal Reflection
How am I establishing a good foundation?

_____

_____

_____

_____

_____

_____

_____

_____

_____

_____

_____

_____

Personal Reflection
How can I maintain balance in my life to make sure I'm being attentive to my spouse?

_____

_____

_____

_____

_____

_____

_____

_____

Day 322

All Scripture is God-breathed and is useful for teaching, rebuking,
correcting and training in righteousness,
2 Timothy 3:16(NIV)

The Word of God is alive and powerful to keepers of His Word. When the word of others fails and comes to naught, God's Word will stand. Jesus said in John 6:63, "the words that I speak, they are spirit, and they are life." With such a powerful source at our disposal, why not let it be a part of our lives? No one has ever read or heard the Word without being affected by it. Jesus is the Word (John 1:1). Use His Word to guide you daily in your marriage decisions. Hide His Word in your heart.

Personal Reflection
How can I apply this passage of scripture and nugget to my marriage?

_____

_____

_____

_____

_____

_____

_____

Day 323

Do not merely listen to the word, and so deceive yourselves. Do what it says.
James 1:22(NIV)

Being genuine in the faith means obeying what the Word of God says. It is a part of your living. Your standards as a Christian and a husband and wife are predicated on your obedience to what God has said. The Word says we are to be committed to each other as husband and wife. If we are faithful to the Word of God, we will be committed to those things that are pleasing to Him convicted of those things that are not like Him. Hearing is useless when we can't apply God's Word to our daily lives. That's why we need to hide the Word in our hearts.

Personal Reflection

How am I remaining obedient to God's original design for marriage?

_____

_____

_____

_____

_____

_____

_____

Day 324

*Therefore, everyone who hears these words of mine and puts them into practice
is like a wise man who built his house on the rock. The rain came down, the streams rose,
and the winds blew and beat against that house; yet it did not fall,
because it had its foundation on the rock.*
Matthew 7:24-25(NIV)

Marriage is founded on the rock of God's unchanging Word. It is insured against destruction. It's not to say that you will not experience some tough days, but who else can sustain you in times of turmoil than the Lord? His Word is accurate and will accomplish what it is purposed to do. It was at creation that God gave marriage purpose. How important is marriage to Him that He instituted marriage even before the church? A marriage will not survive without God at the helm; He is the Creator of marriage. Build your marriage on a rock, and that rock is Jesus. If He is that glue that holds your marriage together, you can be sure that you will bring glory to His name, and He will honor your union together. Marriage is the house that God built!!

Personal Reflection
How have I built the foundation of my marriage?

_____

_____

_____

_____

_____

Day 325

Trust in the Lord with all thine heart; and lean not unto thine own understanding.
In all thy ways acknowledge him, and he shall direct thy paths.
Proverbs 3:5-6 KJV)

The purpose of a blueprint is to serve as a guide or plan for constructing something. It is a pattern or design that can be followed. The ingredients for a good plan, especially for marriage, are given in Proverbs 3. If we would only acknowledge our Creator in all areas of our marriages and lives, He has assured us that we will line up with His blueprint. The Word of God is our road map and blueprint while on planet Earth. Without a plan, our lives would end in chaos. God's Word contains our spiritual design for living. If it is part of our spiritual diets, we find life easier. Applying the Word of God in our lives will result in a lifestyle that will mirror the ways of God.

Personal Reflection

How does God fit into the plans and dreams of my marriage?

_____

_____

_____

_____

_____

_____

Day 326

For our struggle is not against flesh and blood, but against the rulers, against the authorities, against the powers of this dark world and against the spiritual forces of evil in the heavenly realm. Therefore, put on the full armor of God, so that when the day of evil comes, you may be able to stand your ground, and after you have done everything, to stand.
Ephesians 6:12-13(NIV)

As you journey through the experience of marriage, you must be aware of the many plots and schemes that the enemy has to destroy God's intent for a man and woman joined in holy matrimony. Any attempt to taint the very image of God through the marital bond is His priority. Everything about the marital union is designed to reflect the love God has for us; a covenant that binds our hearts in the development of oneness. You must guard your marriage against the wiles and tricks of the enemy by covering yourselves in prayer. Through the wisdom of our God, we can discern these attacks and the great interest that the enemy has in destroying the union of marriage. Know that your fight is not against flesh and blood, but a force so much higher than our finite understanding. Even though the attacks are launched, know that a greater power works in you so that you can withstand all of the fiery darts you may encounter in your marriage.

Personal Reflection
How will I put in the work to make my marriage successful?

_____

_____

_____

_____

Day 327

Do your best to present yourself to God as one approved, a worker who does not need to be ashamed and who correctly handles the word of truth.
2 Timothy 2:15 (NIV)

To use the Word of God as your guide and your source of reference in your marriage, you must know it. It is like wanting to drive a vehicle but never attempting to start the engine. Take pleasure in dedicating time to spend with God in the Word, individually and collectively, especially regarding marriage. As you experience turmoil and struggles in your marriage, God's Word will provide balance to decisions that might affect you as a couple and your family. II Timothy 2:15 is a great reference to studying God's Word.

Personal Reflection
How can I apply this passage of scripture and nugget to my marriage?

_____

_____

_____

_____

_____

_____

_____

Day 328

Unless the Lord builds the house, the builders labor in vain.
Unless the Lord watches over the city, the guards stand watch in vain.
Psalms 127:1 (NIV)

As you chart the course of your marriage, reflect on how God has brought you thus far and the benefits of building a sound relationship with your mate. If you put the work in, your marriage will become a remarkable place of deep trust and knowledge of each other. You will find you can talk without many words and laugh at things nobody else can understand. You will begin to share your worries with the comfort only time can bring to a relationship. Be determined to invest the time and energy in making a lasting love together.

Personal Reflection
How am I consistently working to build a sound relationship with my spouse?

_____

_____

_____

_____

_____

_____

_____

Day 329

He will cover you with his feathers, and under his wings you will find refuge;
his faithfulness will be your shield and rampart.
Psalms 91:4(NIV)

It is so important for all of us to understand that we can do nothing without the help of God. Whenever we think with our finite minds that we can make things happen without Him, we fool ourselves. One of the many targets of the enemy is marriage and the family. You must operate under the covering of God. We can't do this alone. Some couples think a marriage can survive with love alone; sadly, you are mistaken. When your marriage has Christ as the focal point, you can withstand the best and worst times.

Personal Reflection

How can I acknowledge the hand of God in my marriage?

_____

_____

_____

_____

_____

_____

_____

_____

Day 330

For everything that was written in the past was written to teach us,
so that through the endurance taught in the Scriptures
and the encouragement they provide we might have hope.
Romans 15:4(NIV)

The Word of God is essential to the foundation of your marriage. If we have Christ as the rock that we go to when our foundation sometimes seems unstable, we will find He is the glue that will hold us together even in stormy weather. We must purpose in our hearts to stay true to His Word, knowing He can meet our needs. The Word of God has proven to be rock solid. It has been tried and tested since its creation. When everything else around us crumbles, the Word of God will stand. If you can depend on anything else to sustain the both of you through this journey of marriage, hold fast to His will and way for your union. His Word will NEVER fail!

Personal Reflection
How can I apply this passage of scripture and nugget to my marriage?

_____

_____

_____

_____

_____

_____

Day 331

Again, truly I tell you that if two of you on earth agree about anything they ask for, it will be done for them by my Father in heaven.
Matthew 18:19(NIV)

An unselfish attitude is critical to the success of a marriage, taking every opportunity to place your mate before your selfish desires. For our marriage to be effective, we must agree with each other. That means we must kill our flesh and operate in the supernatural. When we operate as one, we will always be aligned with the Word of God. Our wants and desires will align with God's will and not our lustful desires. This also means that we will not compromise, but we will agree without hesitation or reservation that our petitions have been soaked in prayer. We will find much solace in knowing that the Creator of marriage has designed those who partake of marriage to operate in a spirit of oneness. Amos 3:3 asks a critical question, "How can two walk together unless they agree?" We have a spiritual warranty that if we touch and agree, we can make our requests known unto God with the assurance that He will deliver.

Personal Reflection

How do we effectively work as a team to keep our marriage in the will of God?

_____

_____

_____

_____

_____

_____

Day 332

Rejoice always, pray continually, give thanks in all circumstances;
for this is God's will for you in Christ Jesus.
1 Thessalonians 5:16-18 (NIV)

Prayer is one of the most powerful spiritual weapons in a marriage. Couples should always pray for each other as well as pray together. When prayer is a part of what you do, you will find great things happening while bringing unity between you. Take the time and share your prayer requests; it helps when you are touching and agreeing on those things that affect your marriage. Remember that prayer is how you establish communication with your Creator. It's hard to be in a relationship with your spouse and not with God. Prayer is the medium you use to get into the ear of God as He reciprocates His will and way to you and your mate. You will discover that it will release unlimited possibilities in your life. If you have not added prayer to the list of things you do together, today is a mighty good day to start. Watch God work!!

Personal Reflection
How do I apply prayer to every area of my life and marriage?

_____

_____

_____

_____

_____

_____

Day 333

Likewise, the Spirit also helps in our weaknesses. For we do not know what we should pray for as we ought, but the Spirit Himself makes intercession for us with groanings which cannot be uttered.
Romans 8:26(NKJV)

Praying together as a couple takes teamwork. Time should be established where you are touching and agreeing as one. When we do, we are presented with a united front to God, which takes your marriage to a new level. We now operate on a level that God expects us to conduct our lives as a couple. You will find that by praying together, spiritual growth takes place. Those things that would usually tear a marriage apart are easily managed through the power of prayer. Commit yourself this year to a time of praying together. It will lead to a more profound commitment to each other and a healthy relationship.

Personal Reflection

How has my prayer life impacted who I am and my marriage?

_____

_____

_____

_____

_____

_____

Day 334

For this reason, we also, since the day we heard it, do not cease to pray for you, and to ask that you may be filled with the knowledge of His will in all wisdom and spiritual understanding; that you may walk worthy of the Lord, fully pleasing Him, being fruitful in every good work and increasing in the knowledge of God;
Colossians 1:9-10(NKJV)

Love rejoices most in the things that please God. When your mate grows in Christian character, persevering in faith, seeking purity, embracing roles of giving and service, and becoming spiritually responsible in your home. The Bible says we should be celebrating it.

One of marriage's most enjoyable things is witnessing the spiritual growth of two imperfect beings. First, you know that you enter the marriage with different personalities and other imperfections, but the joy of it all is seeing God move in the life of the one you love. Making positive changes in our individual lives is no easy task, but because we pray for the spiritual well-being of each other, we can witness a work that only God can do. When we see these things in the lives of our spouses, thank God, and then let your mate know how you are observing God working in their life.

The spiritual growth of both of you is critical to the longevity of your relationship as husband and wife. When you develop an intimacy with the Creator, you can't help but grow together and become more in love with each other. All of the roadblocks you face will be easier to hurdle because you grow in the Lord. The greatest thing you can do as a couple is surrender your lives and relationship to God's will. As a lifetime lover, make spiritual growth a lifelong commitment; take the time today, count your blessings, and thank God for what He is doing in your marriage.

Personal Reflection

How have we grown spiritually and emotionally in our marriage?

_____

_____

_____

_____

_____

Personal Reflection

How have we included God in the growth of our marriage?

_____

_____

_____

_____

_____

_____

_____

_____

Day 335

A hot-tempered person stirs up conflict,
but the one who is patient calms a quarrel.
Proverbs 15:18 (NIV)

You will have your share of disagreements, but they can be managed without ruining your relationship with each other as long as prayer is in the midst. Be sure to be open with your spouse when you are upset about things. Throwing hints of your displeasure or periods of silence are a waste and are sources of negative communication in your marriage. It would help if you never let your partner resort to the guessing game about what upset you. In the heat of battle, we can many times say things that will hurt each other. Sometimes, our emotions can get the best of us. Remember, best friends don't hurt best friends. Stay calm about who's right and who's wrong! The battle is not about who wins but how we handle the conflict. An excellent place to start is giving the situation to God so He can guide our minds, our tongues, and our thoughts to resolve our disagreements. Make every attempt to close your conflict in a spirit of caring and concern for each other. Pray and let God do it!!

Personal Reflection
How do we work through periods of disagreement and tension?

_____

_____

_____

_____

_____

Day 336

Can two walk together, except they be agreed?
Amos 3:3 (NKJV)

Those of us united in marriage should have the desire as a couple to walk in unity. In this spirit, we share our cares and take all of our petitions before the Lord. To walk together, we must first have a divine connection with God. It is only through our relationship with God that our prayers are heard. If we walk in discord, our prayers and petitions are placed on hold until we have come to common ground, first with God and then with each other. Your commitment to each other to walk in harmony is critical to your relationship. When you are faced with difficult times in your marriage, the question should be asked and answered by both of you, "Am I seeking to walk in harmony or my selfish desires?" If you need to walk harmoniously, now is the time to make things right. Ask for forgiveness and move forward. Never underestimate the power of prayer in your marriage. It will help you see your own issues and love for each other through the eyes of God.

Personal Reflection

How can I demonstrate unity, even in times of dissension?

_____

_____

_____

_____

_____

_____

Day 337

Do not be anxious about anything, but in every situation, by prayer and petition, with thanksgiving present your request to God.
Philippians 4:6 (NIV)

Making prayer a part of your day is vital to the sustainability of your marriage. It should not only be done during a crisis or a time of struggle but whenever you are afforded the time to do so. The Bible tells us that we should always pray because it will enrich the quality of life for our marriage and family. As you face problems in your marriage, prayer will help you to see your issues through the eyes of God. Prayer is a step the both of you take toward strengthening your faith and steering your marriage in the right direction. In addition to praying for each other, pray together regularly. Prayer still works!!

Personal Reflection
How can I apply this passage of scripture and nugget to my marriage?

_____

_____

_____

_____

_____

_____

Day 338

But I cry to you for help, Lord;
in the morning my prayer comes before you.
Psalms 88:13(NIV)

Prayer is a wonderful way to start your day. The fuel will provide you with the energy to go forth through your day. It is that quiet time when you are allowed to speak with God and listen as He speaks to you. David tells us in Psalms 63:1 that it was a precious time for him as He acknowledges the presence of God early in the morning. Rising early in the morning will help you to nurture your relationship with God and to pray for your spouse as you depart your separate ways each day.

Personal Reflection

How can I apply prayer to my everyday process for spiritual uplift?

_____

_____

_____

_____

_____

_____

_____

Day 339

Take delight in the Lord, and he will give you the desires of your heart.
Psalms 37:4(NIV)

It gives me great joy to have such a closeness to God. Whenever we are in His presence, we experience the fullness of His joy. Just having Him in my life makes life worth living. Because of our relationship, there is nothing that He won't do for those He love. Matthew states, "If you, being evil, know how to give good gifts to your children, how much more shall your Father in Heaven give what is good to those who ask Him! Our love for our spouse should be likewise. There is nothing that we won't do to bring joy and happiness to the one we love. As God is with us as His children, so should our affections be for our lover for life.

Personal Reflection
How can I apply this passage of scripture and nugget to my marriage?

_____

_____

_____

_____

_____

_____

_____

Day 340

Finally, brethren, whatever things is true, whatever things are noble,
whatever things are just, whatever things are pure,
whatever things are lovely, whatever things are of good report, if
there is any virtue and if there is anything praiseworthy meditate on these things.
Philippians 4:8(NKJV)

Sometimes, there are moments when you feel that there is nothing that you can think of that can show your lover how in love you are with them. How often do you do that special thing to demonstrate love to your spouse? It's like an annual check-up; you should ensure all parts of your relationship work. Forget about time and cost. Just do it!! Nothing makes your spouse feel more special than a well-thought-out plan to blow their mind.

Personal Reflection
How can I check the pulse of my marriage and relationship?

_____

_____

_____

_____

_____

_____

_____

Day 341

But God demonstrates his own love for us in this:
While we were still sinners, Christ died for us.
Romans 5:8(NIV)

Our love is demonstrated for each other daily as husband and wife. We vowed to love each other despite failures and shortcomings, even when we felt we could have thrown in the towel. When we love on conditions, there are those things we will accept and those we will not. I love you when you .... I love you if you. When we love our spouse unconditionally, we say I love you, even if you fail to do those things I ask or provide me with my selfish desires. Pattern your love for each other after our Creator, who is the essence of love. Unconditional love will put your love for each other through life's obstacle course. Loving unconditionally will build a strong bond between the two of you. If you can love this way, you will find that your love will last and stand the test of time. Love hard!!

Personal Reflection
How can I apply this passage of scripture in demonstrating my love to my spouse?

_____

_____

_____

_____

_____

_____

Day 342

Write the vision and make it plain.
Habakkuk 2:2(NKJV)

The joy of becoming one is seeing your collective dreams and desires fruition. When you share your dreams and aspirations with your spouse, you are facing the realization that you have common goals, plans, and desires. This helps to keep everything about your life together in focus. Your love for each other will help you support each other's dreams. Your dreams together will give clear visions of your marriage and its direction. Sit down and strategize how to accomplish your dreams best, consulting God through prayer.

Personal Reflection
How can I apply this passage of scripture and nugget to my marriage?

_____

_____

_____

_____

_____

_____

_____

_____

Day 343

*My dear brothers and sisters, take note of this: Everyone
should be quick to listen, slow to speak and slow to become angry.
James 1:19(NIV)*

One of the best communicative skills in marriage is listening. When this is done in the spirit of love, you will begin to feel the connection between you and your spouse. It is a good tool for resolving conflict and hearing what your spouse has to say. Your marriage can easily be damaged or dissolved if not done effectively. Make sure you make your partner feel as if what they are about to say is important to you and that you are concerned about their feelings. So, listen attentively to what your spouse is saying to you, not only with your ears but with a heart of love. If you listen well, there is always a message in what is being said.

Personal Reflection
How can I assure my spouse that I am listening and hearing their heart?

_____

_____

_____

_____

_____

_____

Day 344

Give thanks in all circumstances; for this is God's will for you in Christ Jesus.
I Thessalonians 5:18(NIV)

Have you taken the time lately to reflect on who you have had the privilege of sharing your life with and the many storms, struggles, and disappointments you have weathered? Yet, you're still here!! By God's grace, He has sustained both of you and held you up when others counted you out. I don't know about you, but I thank God for my angel. What about you? It's amazing how God can take two unlike personalities and make them one. It can only occur when He is the center of your love and marriage. He will take all of your imperfections as two separate individuals and make them work for your good. Be thankful today for the joy and pleasures you have shared as lifetime lovers. Thank God each day for your heaven-sent angel.

Personal Reflection
How can I apply this passage of scripture and nugget to my marriage?

_____

_____

_____

_____

_____

_____

_____

Day 345

Hold on to wisdom, do not let it go; guard it well, for it is your life.
Proverbs 4:13(NIV)

There may be times in your marriage when you must seriously look at situations as they affect your spouse. You could be tied up with something that is pressing and your spouse may need to have that conversation with you that may be urgent to them, but may not be to you. Even though it may be convenient to talk later, your love for your spouse will allow you to put things on hold and attend to the needs of your lover for life.

Personal Reflection

How can I apply this passage of scripture and nugget to my marriage?

_____

_____

_____

_____

_____

_____

_____

Day 346

Love never fails. But where there are prophecies, they will cease; where there are tongues, they will be stilled; where there is knowledge, it will pass away.
1 Corinthians 13:8(NIV)

A lasting love has a divine quality. Paul compares it to that of a spiritual gift. Love will outlast all of our failures and mistakes. There is nothing more precious in a marriage than the gift of love. Every morning you wake up is a testament to the precious love you share. Each day, we are challenged as Christians to abound in the love that Christ demonstrates. It should also be the example we use when we treat each other with the same love He gives. If God is the foundation of your marriage and your home, then your love will be the blueprint that builds it.

Personal Reflection
How can I apply this passage of scripture and nugget to my marriage?

_____

_____

_____

_____

_____

_____

Day 347

*And this is my prayer: that your love may abound more
and more in knowledge and depth of insight.
Philippians 1:9(NIV)*

One thing you can be sure of is that your love will always be under attack. Many things may come against you, but if your foundation is rock solid, NOTHING will be able to separate you from the love you have for each other. When faced with opposition love will rise to the occasion and dispel anything in its path. This isn't to say that weapons won't be formed, but they won't prosper either. Remember, God is the very essence of Love. When He is part of your relationship, extraordinary things happen. When difficult times occur, love finds a way to persevere. It will give us the motivation to go on; it never fails.

Personal Reflection
How can I apply this passage of scripture and nugget to my marriage?

_____

_____

_____

_____

_____

_____

Day 348

Dear friends, let us love one another, for love comes from God.
Everyone who loves has been born of God and know God.
1 John 4:7(NIV)

Love goes beyond what we can ever imagine. Amid misunderstandings and confusion, love will look beyond what is seen and break those chains that may hold you and your marriage hostage. Love says that I utterly trust you and know the worst and best of you. The effects of love are recorded in I Peter 4:8, Above all, love each other deeply, because love covers a multitude of sin.

Personal Reflection
How deep does your love flow for your lover for life? How is it expressed?

_____

_____

_____

_____

_____

_____

Day 349

Unless the Lord builds the house, the builders labor in vain.
Unless the Lord watches over the city, the guard stand watch in vain.
Psalms 127:1(KJV)

Building your marriage and home on the Word of God will sustain you in anything and all you may encounter. When a house is built, it is placed on a foundation; everything else can go up once the foundation is laid. Having God as your foundation is a sure way that every other addition to your home is part of His divine blueprint. You can rest assured that with God in your blueprints, you will experience a reliable, dependable, and durable foundation that will weather the storms of life. Never depend on yourself (natural/flesh) to build it. It will be similar to building your marriage and relationship on the sand. But when built on that solid rock, it will materialize into a strong rock-solid marriage, making way for a strong family.

Personal Reflection
How can I apply this passage of scripture and nugget to my marriage?

_____

_____

_____

_____

_____

_____

Day 350

But Ruth replied, "Don't urge me to leave you or to turn back from you.
Where you go I will go, and where you stay I will stay.
Your people will be my people and your God my God.
Ruth 1:16(NIV)

As you take on a spouse, several changes must be made in your relationship with your family and your new family. Ruth's statement of commitment reflects the vows made between a man and a woman on their day of marriage. Many struggles exist with couples and their families and in-laws, which could add stress to a working marriage. Healthy marriages recognize that they MUST separate their relationships from their in-laws. There will always be a level of respect, but they too must realize that you are not married to them. Set your boundaries for your outside family and hold them to it. It is always good to maintain healthy relationships with your family, but always keep your distance when it comes to your affairs and relationship with your spouse. Do all you can to protect your spouse from conflict and avoid any times when you can foresee anything that can create a wedge between you and your spouse. Balance will be critical as you seek to establish your relationship with your spouse and create a loving connection with your spouse's family. Make sure God is in the mix.

Personal Reflection
How do I set boundaries for family and friends regarding my marriage?

_____

_____

_____

_____

_____

_____

_____

_____

_____

_____

Personal Reflection
How can I apply this passage of scripture and nugget to my marriage?

_____

_____

_____

_____

_____

_____

_____

Day 351

It always protects, always trusts, always hopes, always perseveres.
1 Corinthians 13:7(NIV)

I remember my wife and I singing to each other at our wedding a song entitled "Endless Love" by Lionel Ritchie. Little did I know then what that meant regarding marriage; a vow of commitment to my spouse until love has ended. It is a love that is everlasting and ongoing. When your love and marriage is interwoven in the love of God, you will find that it will be strengthened both spiritually and individually. When you invest your time and energies in watering your marriage with kindness and patience, it will grow into a love that will endure the trials and tribulations you will encounter. Remember, love bears all things, believes all things, hopes all things, and endures all things." Love NEVER ends.

Personal Reflection
How can I apply this passage of scripture and nugget to my marriage?

_____

_____

_____

_____

_____

_____

_____

Day 352

A covenant is a verbal commitment based on trust, assuring someone that your promise is unconditional and good for life. It is spoken before God out of love for one another. The Bible holds that the marriage of a man and a woman is a covenant. It must be important because Jesus attended the wedding at Cana in Galilee. The Bible's depiction of the Church as the Bride of Christ is significant enough to say that marriage is honorable before the Lord. When we stand before God, we are coming into a covenant with our spouse that means more than possessions, emotions, and intimacy, but a verbal and written agreement that we are in it to win it. It symbolizes your spiritual connection with the One who sanctioned the union between a man and a woman; anything else is NOT of God.

Personal Reflection
How can I best show my commitment to my marriage and my spouse?

_____

_____

_____

_____

_____

_____

Day 353

Therefore, what God has joined together, let not man separate.
Mark 10:9 (NKJV)

The problem with many marriages today is that many consider it a contract rather than a covenant. We can always buy out or nullify a contract, but a covenant is binding. It is vital for those in a marriage or seeking to engage in marriage to realize the seriousness of the process. It is not something that is taken lightly. Serious prayer and thought should be taken when considering this lifetime commitment. Some couples feel marriage is similar to buying a car; when it has run its course, I can trade it for another. NOT SO!! Review your vows. It means even if the tires fall off, we're in it to win!! God's purpose for marriage was that it would be a Holy covenant between God, a man, and a woman.

If we are to save our crumbling families, we MUST revisit marriage and its effect on strong families, strong churches, and strong communities. If we continue to take our vows lightly, we will see the further demise of our country and world. I encourage you to stay the course and choose to prioritize your relationship and marriage with your spouse. Whenever we purchase devices or items that become unworkable, we return them to the manufacturer. God has designed marriage, and HE CAN put the broken pieces back together again.

Personal Reflection
What can I do to respect and commit to God's design for marriage?

_____

_____

_____

_____

_____

_____

_____

_____

_____

_____

Personal Reflection
How can I apply this passage of scripture and nugget to my marriage?

_____

_____

_____

_____

_____

_____

_____

_____

_____

Day 354

But above all things put on love, which is the bond of perfection.
Colossians 3:14 (NKJV)

A covenant has no expiration date. It is till death do us part. As you took your vows, you pledged in covenant that you would faithfully fulfill the responsibility of a husband and a wife. This is a tremendous commitment, one that should not be taken lightly. Come what may, it is a lasting covenant that should endure the best and worst of times. When most of us entered matrimony, we never imagined what would be expected of us.

We took our vows for granted and thought we could live off of love. NOT!! It's more than between the sheets; it requires both parties to endure the hard knocks that can accompany marriage. If both of you work at it each day, it will be nurtured first with the divine love of the Creator of marriage, but you will witness the fruits of your labor of love. Stay faithful to your marriage covenant and be transformed as you understand what God has done, is doing, and will do when you are devoted to that covenant.

Personal Reflection
How can I apply this passage of scripture and nugget to my marriage?

_____

_____

_____

_____

_____

Day 355

I, therefore, the prisoner of the Lord, beseech you to walk worthy of the calling
with which you were called, with all lowliness and gentleness,
with longsuffering, bearing with one another in love,
endeavoring to keep the unity of the Spirit in the bond of peace.
Ephesians 4:1-3(NKJV)

What is essential to all of us who are married is the realization that we are held to a covenant that is bonded in love and loyalty. We are committed to a long-term relationship where our lives and hearts are merged to form the intent of God's design for marriage. Unlike a contract, a covenant is not based on self-gratification or convenience, but a covenant that we form is a spiritual base to bond two hearts becoming one; our spouse's heart can rely on it and the promise and provision of our children and our families can count on it. Your covenant of marriage should be as long as we both shall live. A covenant is unbreakable.

Personal Reflection
How can I apply this passage of scripture and nugget to my marriage?

_____

_____

_____

_____

_____

_____

Day 356

Fulfill my joy by being like-minded, having the same love,
being of one accord, of one mind.
Philippians 2:2 (NKJV)

We believe that a covenant is based upon a relationship, a relationship first with God and then with your spouse. It is committing to experience what God has designed for the marriage despite the circumstances you may face. The fact of the matter is that if you truly love your spouse, you will work hard on your relationship because you are in covenant. We should build our relationship as Jesus spoke of; build upon an unmovable rock. We are in it for the long haul when we genuinely love each other. In building our covenant relationship, we are constantly validating our love for each other and helping to do those things to nurture our love. Loving someone is not giving up or giving in but giving everything that's needed to keep your marriage alive and vibrant.

Personal Reflection
How can I apply this passage of scripture and nugget to my marriage?

_____

_____

_____

_____

_____

_____

Day 357

That Christ may dwell in your hearts through faith; that you,
being rooted and grounded in love.
Ephesians 3:17(NKJV)

Love is a holy treasure to trade in for another and a powerful bond not to be broken without dire consequences. Fasten your love afresh on the one the Lord has given you to cherish, prize, and honor. Your life together is before you. Dare to take hold of it and never let go.

Personal Reflection
How can I apply this passage of scripture and nugget to my marriage?

_____

_____

_____

_____

_____

_____

_____

Day 358

As water reflects the face, so one's life reflects the heart.
Proverbs 27:19(NIV)

The Bible tells us that where your heart is, there will your treasure be also. Love is not enough. There are a lot of things to consider such as entrusting your spouse to the health of your heart. If we are committed to each other, we will trust our hearts in the hands of someone who delights in making us happy. They would love us unconditionally and can envision a commitment till death do us part. Continue to love each other with everlasting love, and remember that when two hearts are joined, love can get in.

For he is the kind of person who is always thinking about the cost.
"Eat and drink," he says to you, but his heart is not with you.
Proverbs 23:7(NIV)

Personal Reflection
How can I apply this passage of scripture and nugget to my marriage?

_____

_____

_____

_____

_____

_____

Day 359

Those who trust in themselves are fools, but those who walk in wisdom are kept safe.
Proverbs 28:26(NIV)

We go into a marriage trusting in our spouses to fulfill our wants and desires, but the secret is that you first put your trust in God. It means trusting in the Lord with your whole heart, every event, disappointment, every prayer, with unshakable faith and conviction that God will honor His Word and that you can trust Him. Our problem sometimes is that we put our trust in people and things that have proven to be full of faults and imperfections. Trust Him so that He can run your life and your marriage. The secret to it all lies in the power of the Holy Spirit within you. Before you think of giving anybody your heart, trust it first with God. You won't go wrong.

Personal Reflection
How can I apply this passage of scripture and nugget to my marriage?

_____

_____

_____

_____

_____

_____

Day 360

And so, we know and rely on the love God has for us.
God is love. Whoever lives in love lives in God, and God in them.
1 John 4:16(NIV)

Love for each other should mirror the love that Christ modeled for us all. Despite all our sins and shortcomings, He loved us so much to give of Himself as that sacrifice. This kind of love means that the husband seeks to go the distance to care for, nurture, and look out for his bride's best needs. For the wife, that undeserved love means she will enjoy seeing her husband grow spiritually and emotionally. Your love is like a coin, it has two sides, giving and receiving. God has created us with the capacity to be on the receiving end and can provide in return. Today, affirm your love for each other by merely saying, I love you.

Personal Reflection
How can I apply this passage of scripture and nugget to my marriage?

_____

_____

_____

_____

_____

_____

Day 361

If we live in the Spirit, let us also walk in the Spirit.
Galatians 5:25(NKJV)

One of the musts for a couple is to have that connection with God. You are incapable of directing yourself. Our sinful nature will lead us away from anything aligned with God's blueprint for our lives and marriage. Within you lies a spiritual GPS capable of guiding both of you in those things of God. He will guide you in all truth. John 16:13(KJV) He, the Holy Spirit, will guide you into all truth: for He shall not speak of Himself, but whatsoever He shall hear, that shall He speak, and He will show you things to come. He has His hand on you and your marriage for a specific purpose: to fulfill His marriage design and bring Him glory.

Personal Reflection
How has my walk with God influenced my life and marriage?

_____

_____

_____

_____

_____

_____

Day 362

I can do all this through Him who gives me strength.
Philippians 4:13(NIV)

If we practiced Christ's unconditional love, there would be no cause for separation and divorce. Maybe your spouse has somehow changed and is different from when you were married. Yet, you have this persevering spirit in you to go all the way. Stay in it to win it. It is the same type of love God has for us, and we should make every effort to model that love with our spouses. It will become a little easier for us when we are in a relationship with God. I can't emphasize enough the importance of having God in the formula. With Him, we can do things that would blow our minds in the natural, but in the spiritual, we know that it is in Him that we can experience a life that will bring Glory to Him.

Personal Reflection
How can I apply this passage of scripture and nugget to my marriage?

_____

_____

_____

_____

_____

_____

Day 363

Again, I say unto you, that if two of you shall agree on earth as touching anything that they shall ask, it shall be done for them of my Father which is in heaven.
Matthew 18:19(KJV)

For marriage to be sustained and endure the best and worst of times, it must have a foundation built on communication. The survival of your marriage is contingent upon how you communicate with each other. Be sure that you first speak with God and that there are periods in which you actively pray individually and collectively. There must be a sense of intimacy and closeness which is the evidence that you are on the same team. You will be able to move together by establishing the plans and vision for your marriage and how you can move it together. The Word of God assures us of this.

Personal Reflection
How can I apply this passage of scripture and nugget to my marriage?

_____

_____

_____

_____

_____

_____

Day 364

But God has put the body together, giving greater honor to the parts that lacked it,
so that there should be no division in the body,
but that its parts should have equal concern for each other.
1 Corinthians 12:24-25(NIV)

The survival of your marriage is contingent upon the teamwork between a husband and a wife. Our Creator, from the beginning, had a relationship in mind. It requires that everything in your marriage involves you standing together in unity. In your marriage, every decision, whether financial, career change, child-rearing, or spiritual growth, should involve working together as a team. It helps to dispel the many forces of the enemy that may come against your marriage. Your loyalty to each other is critical to the teamwork needed in your marriage. You will never be able to experience victory in your marriage if you are not working on it together. Make it a TEAM EFFORT.

Personal Reflection
How are we working together to make our marriage work?

_____

_____

_____

_____

_____

_____

Day 365

The glory of this latter house shall be greater than of the former, saith the Lord of hosts: and in this place will I give peace, saith the Lord of hosts.
Haggai 2:9(KJV)

As you approach each new dawning, reflect upon the situations you encountered and celebrate the goodness of God as He has helped sustain your marriage through the many tests and trials. Leave all those things that held your marriage hostage in the past. Celebrate where God will take your marriage moving forward. Each new day brings new mercies through new possibilities and new-found ways to fulfill God's purpose for your lives together. Celebrate each other more and resolve to continue to make each other happy. Keep the focus of your marriage God-centered, and you will witness all the promises to ensure your marital journey's success.

Personal Reflection
How can I reflect on the goodness of God in past disagreements?

_____

_____

_____

_____

_____

Personal Reflection
How can I apply this passage of scripture and nugget to my marriage?

_____

_____

_____

_____

_____

_____

_____

_____

_____

_____

_____

_____

_____

_____

Wedding Anniversary Nugget

So, they are no longer two but one flesh:
Therefore, what God has joined together, let no one separate.
Matthew 19:6 (NIV)

Today marks your wedding anniversary day, the special day you took your vows. It is a day to reflect on the fact that you have survived as a couple, despite its stormy waters and sometimes rocky moments. God has remained a constant in your relationship and a significant part of a milestone celebration that becomes another chapter in the memories of marriage that God ordained for a man and a woman. Today is your day to renew your commitment to each other and that it is a product of love; two people who have vowed to cherish each other for the rest of your lives.

By God's grace, you are still standing, and by his guidance, you continue this journey called marriage. Vow to keep the flame burning forever; loving each other in good times and in bad times. We pray that you both will hold true to your vows no matter how strong the waves and storms you face. Celebrate the love, growth, trust, tolerance, and partnership you share. Let your lives together be an encouragement and a source of inspiration to those you are associated with. Love hard and keep God in the forefront of everything in your marriage. Happy Anniversary!!!!!

Blessings to you both as you continue your marital journey.
Rev. Danny & Rhoda Whitfield

About the Authors

Rev. Danny and Rhoda Whitfield met at Florida A&M University, where they became college sweethearts. Through their 40-plus years of marriage, they have experienced many bumps and bruises, but they have stayed on the course of their marital journey. God birthed a new passion in them to share with other married and prospective couples. They wish to see every married couple successful in their relationship by making them aware of helpful tips to maintain their marriage.

Rev. Whitfield is presently an Administrative Pastor at the Tabernacle Missionary Baptist Church in Tallahassee, Florida. He has a B.S. degree in Music Education and a Master of Education in Educational Leadership. He is a 2016 graduate of the Interdenominational Theological Center in Atlanta (Morehouse School of Religion) with a Master of Divinity degree. He retired as an educator and administrator of thirty-four years with Leon County School System. He has acquired a heart for the liberation and transformation of God's people. Utilizing his "people" skills and training in Pastoral Care, Rev. Whitfield seeks to connect with couples, young and old, in the exploration of being "lovers for life." It is through the process of hard work that couples can learn to communicate with each other better and allow God to be the foundation of their sacred union.

Rhoda Whitfield graduated in education and is a retired educator. She believes in order to maintain a successful marriage you have to nurture your marriage daily. From January 2014 through January 2015, she was Co-host of Women of Wisdom Marriage Empowerment. They were featured on "A Moment of Inspiration" television segment and recorded monthly telecasts on marital topics to enhance a marriage. In 2016 to 2020, she began writing a blog for an online magazine, Purpose Driven Woman entitled "Just Simply Saying". She is a Marriage Coach with a wealth of wisdom concerning marriage. She is the author of five previously published books.

The Whitfields believe that it is essentially important for God to be at the forefront of the marriage. They further believe that married couples should follow God's original intent for marriage so that they can receive God's blessings upon their union. As husband and wife, we are in a covenant with Him and should take everything regarding our marriage to Him in prayer. They have a weekly radio segment, "Marriage Takes Work," on Hallelujah 95.3 FM, that inspires couples to be strengthened through their candid transparency. They conduct retreats, workshops, and seminars upon request, which assist couples with their everyday questions and struggles.

Other Resources by Danny and Rhoda Whitfield

Books:
A Well-Rounded Love Affair: More Than Between the Sheets
Where Did You Go?
Where Did You Go? Supplemental Guide and Journal
I'm Just Simply Saying: Marriage Takes Work
I'm Just Simply Saying: Marriages Takes Work Couple's Workbook

All books can be purchased on Amazon.

Coming Soon:
The Last 48 Hours

Workshops and Trainings:
Marriage Workshops

Counseling:
Pre-marital Counseling
Marital Counseling
Grief Counseling

Contact Us:
dannyandrhodawhitfield.com
Instagram: @marriagetakeswork2
Facebook: @marriagetakeswork
Facebook: @DannyandRhodaWhitfield
Email: marriagetakeswork2016@gmail.com

To request a workshop and training or to learn more about our counseling services email us at marriagetakeswork2016@gmail.com

Made in the USA
Columbia, SC
16 January 2025

51970543R00404